ATYIDAE

22

THE MASQUE OF CAPRI

EDWIN CERIO

THE MASQUE OF CAPRI

EDIZIONI LA CONCHIGLIA

Line Drawings by Laetitia Cerio:
pages 10 - 65 - 192 - 207

Edizioni La Conchiglia - Via le Botteghe 12 - Capri (Napoli)
Phone/Fax 0818376577-0818378199
e-mail: laconchiglia.capri@libero.it
On the front cover: painting by Carmine Giardiello

CONTENTS

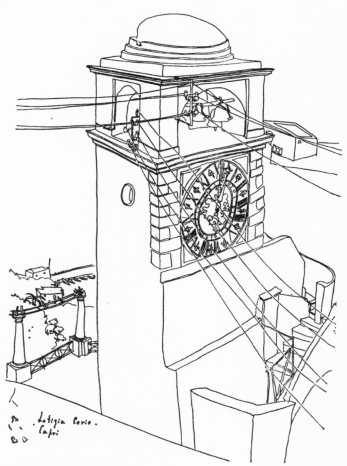

Letizia Cerio.
Capri

The Campanile of Capri

TO
SILVIA

CHAPTER I

FROM MYTH TO HISTORY

The Island of Capri lies at the southern tip of the Bay of Naples. Its story begins in the days of the gods and heroes, and if we want to find our way to historical times we must read the tales of Homer and Virgil, and use the *Odyssey* and the *Aeneid* as our guides. At Capri, where geography and fantasy merge imperceptibly into poetry, the journeys of Ulysses and Aeneas are spread out before our eyes. It is a simple matter to retrace, or better still, to invent the routes these heroes followed, while all around, within the horizon, in Lucania, Campania and Latium, lie places still known by their ancient names.

Simply by looking out from the northern slopes of Capri, we can see, beyond Ischia and Cape Misenum, the hills behind Formia where dwelt a race of cannibals and robbers mentioned by Homer, the Laestrigonians, who conquered the littoral and the adjacent islands—the Pontines, Ischia, Procida and Capri—and peopled them with savage tribes. It was they who attacked and practically destroyed the fleet of Ulysses as he was hastening, though not unduly, back to his home and his Penelope. Eleven out of twelve ships were sunk and their crews torn to bits, and Ulysses was glad to make his escape with his one surviving ship, and move on northwestward, towards the island of Aeaea, or rather the Promontorio Circeo, the promontory of Circe, which even today, seen emerging from the distant haze, can be mistaken for an island.

Ulysses will be appearing again in our story; but for the moment let us leave him to the attentions of the formidable enchantress Circe, and move southward from Latium to Campania, recalling as we go the varied mythical and historical associations of the landscape.

Hidden from sight by Cape Misenum is Cumae, where the Sibyl showed to Aeneas the way to the Underworld. Entering the Bay of Naples through the Procida Channel, we come upon Misenum, site of the villas of Mark Antony and Lucullus. Here begins the most famous chain of pleasure-resorts in the Campania Felix: first, la Piscina Mirabile, on the Mare Morto; then Bacoli, the former Bauli, renowned for its magnificent beach and the adjacent ruins of the tomb of Agrippina, the villas of Hortensius, Caesar, Crassus and Piso, and the remains of an ancient theatre; next Baia; and then the Lucrine Lake, not far from Lake Avernus; while all along the coast are scattered the remains of other famous villas, such as those of Pompey and Cicero, and, near the Serapeum of Pozzuoli, the villa of Sulla.

Off the little island of Nisida, the ancient *Nesis*, lies *lo scoglio di Virgilio*, Virgil's rock; then, a few miles eastward, Cape Posillipo, called after the villa of Vedius Pollio, *Pausilypon*. This promontory marks the beginning of Naples, the "New City" established after the foundation of Cumae, and built on the strand which, legend says, had witnessed the death of one of the Sirens, Parthenope. Her memory is still revered in the city, and her image has long been a favourite Neapolitan lucky charm.

Due north from the port of Capri, on the other side of the Bay, stands the Castel dell'Ovo, once the site of the Greek settlement Megaris, and built on the remains of one of the most luxurious villas of Lucullus. Travelling eastward from Naples, the eye lights upon another cluster of Greco-Roman cities, or their modern successors: Herculaneum, between Portici and Resina, at the foot of Monte Somma (as the outer cone of Vesuvius is properly called); then, behind the mountain, Ottaiano, formerly *Octavianum*, so called after the villa of Octavian, where the famous emperor entertained some of the greatest figures of the Augustan age. A little beyond Torre Annunziata is Pompeii; and farther inland, Boscotrecase, site of the ancient and renowned *Sylva mala*, from whose vineyards came the exquisite "lacrime", or wines, so dear to the Romans, of which the *Lachryma Christi* is the only modern survivor of comparable strength. Not far away is Boscoreale, the hunting reserve of the Angevin kings of Naples, where stood the Roman villa whose ruins yielded the hoard of silver vases of Alexandrine manufacture now in the Louvre.

Behind the Monti Lattari, a spur of the Apennines running out towards Capri, lie Castellammare, the old *Stabia*, and Sorrento. The name Sorrento is said to derive from *Surrentum*, from the Sirens, and the town still remembers with pride its Greco-Roman origins, to which a variety of ruins bears witness. From Capri can be seen the ruins of the Villa of Vedius Pollio on the tip of the Sorrentine peninsula, and the site, and unfortunately only the site, of one of the largest and most famous temples of antiquity, the temple of Minerva or Athene, on the Punta della Campanella, which was called by the Greeks the Promontory of Athene, and by the Romans *promontorium Minervae*. The name of a little bay on the coast of the peninsula, *la Marinella di Ierate*, still retains a trace of the hieratic, sacred nature of the spot.

It is tempting to pursue still further these memories of the past along the coastline of Amalfi and the fabled shores of Lucania. On the coast road from Salernum we might meet the Roman legions, marching to the conquest of the south, and leaving in their wake settlements which mark the stages of their glorious march, Picentia, Eborum, Acerronia... Across the mouth of the River Sele (the Latin *Silarus*) rise the ruins of Paestum; beyond, Punta Licosa, with its reminder of another of the Sirens, Leucosia, who died, they say, for love of Ulysses. Beyond again is Cape Palinurus, where Aeneas' beloved pilot met his death.

But topographically this is as far as we can go. Geography has brought us back to myth, and we must rejoin Ulysses whom we left on the island of Circe. We pick up the story when he is about to leave the island, and to resume the complicated journey which will lead him back, eventually, to Ithaca. Before he goes, Circe warns him of a great danger which he will meet, not far away, if he listens to the song of the Sirens as he passes their island or yields to their charms.

Which of the many islands, or even which of the many rocks, strewn along the route of Ulysses, is to be identified with the haunt of the Sirens? Off the coast of Amalfi, beyond the promontory of Minerva, there is a group of small islands called I Galli, which in old nautical charts are marked as *Le Sirenuse*, and this has led to their being acclaimed by some as the *Sirenum Scopuli*, mentioned by the old geographers. But the poem speaks of the honey-voiced nymphs displaying their charms on a flat-topped rock, the "Antemoessa" (or flowery meadow), stretching out to sea. Long dissertations by the most authoritative modern sirenologists, together with the evidence of poets, historians and geographers of all times, not to mention the weighty opinion of the local hoteliers and tourist organisations, all lead to the same conclusion: this "Antemoessa" can only be the *Scoglio delle Sirene*, or Sirens' Rock, at the Piccola Marina, on the south coast of Capri, and Capri therefore the fabulous island of Homer's poem. So going for a swim at the famous beach, we have only to close our eyes to picture the dramatic scene.

16

As Ulysses'ship sights Capri, the favourable wind called up by Circe dies away, perhaps as a result of some new, local spell, while from the shore rises the melodious song of the magic creatures, fatal to sailors. The men take down the sails, and the ship speeds on under oars. Ulysses plugs the ears of the oarsmen with wax, and has himself tied to the mast, and thus they pass beyond the Faraglioni and out of danger. The boat disappears to the south, passes within sight of Stromboli, slips between Scylla and Charybdis—and leaves the waters of Capri for ever.

But Capri, the probable site of one of the most poetic legends of antiquity, was itself destined to provide evidence in the shape of fossils for a rational explanation of the story. Overlooking the Sirens' Rock, and not far from the Piccola Marina, is a great natural archway in the hillside. This terminates in a cave, the *Grotta delle Felci* or Fern Grotto, closed on its southern side by a huge boulder which came away from Monte Solaro and fell to its present position thousands of years ago, thus forming a perfect example of the typical prehistoric dwelling known as *abri-sous-roche* or rock shelter. Excavations, first carried out about 1880, and continued at intervals during the ensuing sixty years, have proved that the Grotto was in continual occupation by early islanders from the Neolithic to the Bronze Age. Among the fossilised remains of meals were recognised the bones of *Homo Sapiens*, split so as to get at the marrow—bones, presumably of sailors, lured on to the rocks by the songs and seductions of the womenfolk of the island, and eaten by the cannibal Laestrigonians, the ancient inhabitants of Capri.

Perhaps it was on these shores that Ulysses, who had already tried the herb "moly" offered him by the god Hermes as an antidote to the spells of Circe, also tasted the lotus leaves of oblivion, and then sang the praises of their magic properties on his return to Ithaca.

17

For in the twilight of the past, when history is not to be distinguished from myth, there set out from far-off Acarnania, a district on the mainland of Greece opposite Ithaca, an expedition of Teleboans, "men who have travelled far from their native land", led by their king Telon, desirous of oblivion. According to Virgil, Telon, when an old man, landed on Capri (called by Virgil *saxosa Telonis insula*, the rocky isle of Telon) and founded there a new and prosperous kingdom. Telon had much to forget—no less than twenty wives left behind in Acarnania; but he seems to have succeeded very well, for he spent his time in dalliance with the nymph Sebethis, who bore him a son, Oebalus, a great brigand who conquered much land in the neighbourhood of Capri, and later fought against Aeneas.

It has been suggested that the journey of Ulysses could have been traced on the charts of any Phoenician master-mariner. Certainly the mariners of Tyre and Sidon, "the Semites of the Sea", settled along the whole of the Mediterranean seaboard, from the Syrtes to the Spanish Sea, and may even have ventured beyond the Pillars of Hercules. We find them in Spain as far as Cartagena, in the Balearic Islands, in Sardinia and Sicily, and they also make an appearance in the Bay of Naples. Megaris, Castel dell'Ovo together with Santa Lucia on the sea-front of Naples, was probably a Phoenician colony before the Greeks set foot in the area, while the Cala di Limbo, in Anacapri, the terminal point of a rock road which Amedeo Maiuri describes as Homeric, was the site, if not of a Phoenician colony, at least of one of their trading stations. Greek authors, however, say little or nothing of their dreaded competitors and rivals, and Dionysius of Halicarnassus, the best informed historian of the Greek colonies in the Campania, consistently ignores the Phoenicians. At Capri, the only surviving trace of their presence is to be found in the names of two species of plants disseminated in the path of Phoenician civilisation: the date-palm, *Phoenix dactylifera*, and the juniper, *Juniperus phoenicea*, native of the eastern Mediterranean seaboard, which supplied first the Phoenicians then the Greeks and then the inhabitants of Anacapri with a favourite source of firewood.

Those who like to think that Capri was first settled by the Phoenicians derive its name from the Hebrew *Capraim*, meaning two villages, and referring to the existence of two separate communities on the island, a fact confirmed by the first reliable geographic reference to Capri in the pages of Strabo: "*Caprearum duo antiquitus oppidula nunc vero unum quod Neapolitani occupavere*" ("In ancient times there were two settlements on Capri; now there is only one, which the Neapolitans have occupied"). More weight, however, attaches to the derivation of the name from the Greek word *Kàpros*, wild boar, the most common animal in the prehistoric fauna of the island. On the other hand, the derivation of *Caprae* from the Latin *capra*, goat, can be dismissed as worthless, for when the island became a possession of the Caesars, and Latin began to be spoken there, it had already had a Greek name for many centuries.

Water-colour in Indian ink by Rose O'Neill

Chapter II

IMPERIAL CAPRI

On the Ides of March in the year 44 B.C., Julius Caesar was stabbed to death in the Senate. On that day Republican Rome died too, and with the genealogy of the Julio-Claudian family the Empire begins.

Caesar had adopted as his heir Caius Octavius, who, on Caesar's death, assumed by law the name of Caius Julius Caesar Octavianus, which he changed in 27 B.C. to Augustus. On his return from Apollonia in Albania, where he had been studying literature and military affairs, the young man broke his journey at Naples, and stayed with his step-father Philip at Cumae. While here he visited Cicero in his villa, showing much respect and honour to the famous Roman orator and lawyer. From this visit we can date the great love of the future founder of the Empire for Campania; for, immediately after his accession to the throne, he began, in the words of Suetonius, to visit its shores and its islands. So begins the Augustan age, and Campania becomes Imperial.

One of its most distinguished residents was the great poet Virgil, who, after his journey to Brindisi with Horace, left Rome and settled in Naples, where he had studied Greek as a youth; he also spent some time at Nola. When Augustus returned from Asia, in 29 B.C., it was at Atella, a town in Campania famous for its farces, that Virgil read him the *Georgics*. Augustus, flattered by the praise given to his military glory in the poem, commissioned Virgil to write a longer poem in praise of Aeneas, whom he considered to be the founder of his family, the *gens Julia*. When Virgil, on returning with Augustus from a visit to Greece, died at Brindisi, he expressed the wish to be buried at Naples, and composed his own epitaph: "Mantua bore me, the Calabrians stole me, now Parthenope holds me; I sang of pastures, fields and great leaders".

The frequent sojourns of Augustus in Campania were enlivened by the company of other less important poets, and also by the hospitality of wealthy and generous neighbours in their villas. Augustus took a particular delight in the symposiums in Vedius Pollio's villa at Posillipo, where the genial host gathered around his Imperial guest the noblest spirits of the age.

The date of Augustus' first visit to Capri is not known for certain; but it is usually given as 29 B.C., on his return from Egypt after the battle of Actium. According to Suetonius, he took a fancy to the island at the sight of an ancient and withered ilex which suddenly burst into leaf in his presence. The happy augury (or perhaps it was a clever trick on the part of the crafty islanders) made him decide to exchange with the Republic of Naples his private domain, Ischia, for their Capri, which, though smaller, was more Greek and thus more attractive to his hellenised taste. After recording this event, the historians of Augustus go on to stress the ancient institutions and customs of Capri, and its civilised life, which was to be the solace of the Emperor on his frequent visits. Capri, according to Suetonius, was the seat of an ancient Ephebeum or academy for young men, where men of letters used to assemble, and youths meet for literary discussion and gymnastic exercises, according to the Greek custom.

Augustus was also delighted to find on the island "not a few monuments which for excellence and antiquity are outstanding". Strabo assures us that in his private capacity, Augustus did much for Capri, and provided it with fine buildings; and it was perhaps the architectural evidence of Greek greatness and civilisation which encouraged him in his schemes. Be that as it may, he certainly adorned the island with new and grandiose buildings, irrigated it by means of large-scale hydraulic projects, and planted it with gardens and glades so that it became the most precious jewel in the Imperial crown. The famous rock steps which connect the lower town to the upper hamlet, "Ana-Capri", though usually attributed to the Phoenicians, are definitely the work of Augustus. His too are the sumptuous villas and temples of Palazzo a Mare and Damecuta, and probably also Villa Jovis, destined to become under his successor the second Palatine of Imperial Rome.

It was at Capri, according to Suetonius, his most detailed historian, that Augustus assumed the pose of the prince weary of honours and of glory, who yearned for the simple life, without luxury or ostentation. There is a story that he made his granddaughter Julia raze to the ground a country house which she had built with too great cost and magnificence. He himself would not have statues or valuable pictures, says Suetonius, but preferred to adorn his "simple" dwellings with "such things, as for their antiquitie and rareness were notable: *qualia sunt Capreis immanium belluarumn ferarumque membra praegrandia, quae dicuntur gigantium ossa et arma Heroum*—of which sort were at Caprae the huge members of monstrous fishes (as whales, whirlpooles, etc.) and wilde beasts: the bones that are saide to bee of Gyants, and the armour of the demigods and worthies in olde time".

And here, in this somewhat obscure passage of Augustus' biographer Suetonius, we catch the echo of a famous controversy which raged among historians and critics of the nineteenth century, only to be resolved at the beginning of the present century by a memorable palaeontological discovery.

What were these "bones that are saide to bee of Gyants, and the armour (or arms) of the demigods and worthies in olde time", which Augustus collected and preserved at Capri as interesting rarities? Salomon Reinach, the high priest of nineteenth-century archaeology, came to the conclusion in his work *Le Musée de l'Empereur Auguste*, that the *arma Heroum* must have been chipped stone implements of the Neolithic period—the sort of thing the Romans called *cerauniae*, and considered as the products of thunderbolts, meteors and other heavenly agencies. Such was the authority of the French archaeologist that this theory was considered sound and was accepted by most people. Towards the end of the century, however, prehistory moved even farther back into the mists of antiquity with the discovery of Chelles in Northern France of the oldest-known artefacts, the almond-shaped flint weapons, or *coups de poing*. The Old Stone Age had been discovered, and Palaeolithic Man appeared on the scene. In Capri in 1906, after thirty years' incessant research, a local doctor and naturalist, Ignazio Cerio, discovered at the Quisisana diggings the first signs of Palaeolithic Man in Italy: the Chellean *coup de poing* and other products of Palaeolithic craftsmanship. They were found in association with the fossilised remains of the great Pleistocene mammals and thus enabled the first appearance of man on Capri to be fixed at the beginning of the Quaternary period (about 500,000 B.C.).

With the discovery of these huge ancient bones and large flint tools we have at last the *gigantium ossa* and the *arma Heroum* which Augustus, the first, if unwitting, palaeontologist, collected and preserved in the museum attributed to him by Salomon Reinach.

The discovery after nineteen centuries of these "things, as for their antiquitie and rareness were notable" also gave the lie to Mommsen's statement that "there was no evidence for the existence in Italy of a race anterior to the development of primitive husbandry and the fusion of metals". Caesar Augustus had found and preserved in his villas on Capri evidence showing the existence of a race of men in Italy five hundred thousand years before the creation of the Roman Empire.

Although there is no exact tally of the visits of Augustus to Capri, he must have frequented the island for over forty years, from the end of his Egyptian campaign until his death, throughout the happy period of the "Peace of Augustus". Anecdotes about his residence on Capri illustrate the pleasant traits of his character, his delight in living in such congenial surroundings, and the liberty with which he allowed the inhabitants to follow their Greek laws and customs. His favourite and friend was Masgaba, the architect of his villas, to whom he gave the Greek nickname of *Ctisi*, the builder. The Emperor used joikingly to describe him as the founder of a colony of "do-nothings", who lived on the neighbouring "island" of Apragopolis. By this he may have meant Anacapri, or perhaps the large rock now called Il Monacone, where supposed traces of Masgaba's tomb have been found. One night, noticing Apragopolis lit up by torches in honour of his dead friend, Augustus composed on the spur of the moment a line of poetry in Greek, and turning to his fellow diners, asked them if they knew who the author was. Thrasyllus, like a good courtier, replied that, though unknown to him, the line was clearly by a good poet—a reply which caused great amusement to Augustus. Such were the innocent pleasures with which the Emperor beguiled his time on Capri. Sometimes, we are told, he would take his leisure at the Ephebeum, entertaining at sumptuous banquets the most handsome young men and the prettiest girls, and enjoying himself very much.

The Emperor reached old age without having any direct heirs, and in 6 B.C. he decided to reward Tiberius for his successes in Germany, and at the same time fulfil the hopes of the Romans, by associating him in the affairs of the Empire, and thus preparing him for the succession. At Nola in the year A.D. 14, shortly after leaving Capri with his adopted heir, Augustus fell ill for the last time. He made a long speech to Tiberius, his political last will and testament, and before dying gathered around him his faithful friends and asked them for their applause if he had played his part well. He died in the arms of his wife, saying to her: "Livia, do not forget our life together! *Vale!*".

Of the twenty-three years of his rule, A.D. 14-37, Tiberius passed the last ten at Capri. When he settled there, he was already an old man, almost sixty-nine. His private life, though full of misfortune, had been blameless, and his public life had been entirely devoted to the service of his country, both in the field and in the council chamber. He had borne with honour the dignity of the tribune's office, and had reached old age with the reputation of being a first-class magistrate, a strict and upright administrator, and a wise and successful general.

If Augustus had founded the Empire, it was Tiberius who consolidated it, strengthened its weak links and ruled it at the height of its splendour. In the west and north, the Empire now stretched from Lusitania, in Portugal, to Gaul, Britain, Germany and Rhaetia; its eastern frontiers ran from Dacia to Thrace, Armenia, Assyria, Mesopotamia and Syria; in Africa, its possessions included Egypt, Libya, Numidia and Mauretania. In fact, it comprised what was at that time the whole of the known world. By taking up his residence on Capri, Tiberius made the island the hub and nerve-centre of the whole complicated structure. This justifies the words of a forgotten philosopher, Giovanni Bovio of

Naples, who, in a play called *Christ at the Feast of Purim*, makes one of the characters say: "The law of the world is conceived at Capri, sold at Rome, and imposed on the whole Earth". It also explains the proud description of Capri as "a small island indeed, but once the rival of Rome, and worthy to house the Caesars".

Many classical authors, some contemporary, others of a later period, mention Capri and the Emperor Tiberius; and all agree in recognising in him the qualities which had induced Augustus to adopt him and leave him the succession. Among these authors are: Philo Judaeus, Phaedrus, Seneca, Pliny, Josephus, Juvenal, Quintilian, Statius and Plutarch. Not until eighty years after the death of Tiberius did the *Annals* of Tacitus appear.

Tacitus begins by paying the necessary tribute to the climate and scenery of the island: "The temperature of the climate is mild in winter, from the shelter of a mountain, which intercepts the rigour of the winds: its summers are refreshed by gales from the west, and are rendered delightful from the wide ekpanse of sea which the island commands; before the fiery eruption of Mount Vesuvius had changed the face of the country, there was also a prospect of the lovely Bay of Naples". But this is only a framework skilfully designed to set off what is to follow. Into this setting Tacitus places the conventional portrait of the old libertine steeped in vice, who has shut himself up on an inaccessible rock so that he can perpetrate the blackest crimes, give free rein to his lust, and indulge in the most refined and incredible cruelties. This is nothing more nor less than the faithful reproduction of the classical description of the "Tyrant", based on the model taught in all the schools of rhetoric and with all the prescribed ingredients: the secretiveness, the sensuality, the true face of the evil-doer who has torn off the mask of hypocrisy; in short, all the symptoms of *dementia senilis*, aggravated

27

by solitude and embittered by remorse in old age. This Tiberius, born in the *Annals* eighty years after the death of the real Tiberius, is completed by the portrait of the tyrant drawn in the *Lives of the Caesars* by Suetonius, that pleader of lost causes and master of rhetoric who passed for the biographer of the twelve Caesars, but who was in fact merely the retailer of gossip concerning their private lives. Out of the materials contained in these two versions of the history of Tiberius—versions which aimed at ingratiating their authors with the successors of the great Emperor, and satisfying posterity's taste for scandal—was fabricated the so-called "Orgy of Capri", which helped to give Capri such a bad reputation, and, at the same time, to make the island's fortune.

It is to Voltaire that we owe the first attack on the structure of lies erected on the basis of the two Tiberian classics. But it was left to a humble contemporary of his, G.M. Secondo, Governor of Capri, to ask, with much good sense, in his *Relazione storica dell'Antichità, Rovine e Residui di Capri*, why it was necessary for Tiberius to choose Capri as the scene of his debauchery, when nothing prevented him from doing what he liked at Rome. This theme is also taken up in some letters by Engelbach, published anonymously in *Naples and the Campagna Felice*, by R. Ackermann (London, 1815).

From these first cautious attempts to rehabilitate Tiberius has sprung a vast literature concerned with white—washing his memory. At the beginning of this century, a mayor of Capri even went so far as to found an international society, the *Société des Amis de Tibère*, and to declare 16 March, the date of Tiberius' death, a day of municipal mourning, marking it by a funeral banquet vividly described in a chapter of Louis Golding's *Sunward*. However, the culminating point in the campaign to rehabilitate Tiberius was reached with the proposal to affix to the Campanile of the Piazza of Capri a memorial tablet—offered by a rich American—in which were set out the civil and military virtues, the Christian charity, I might almost say the homely qualities, of the island's gentle benefactor. Justly perturbed by the loss the island would suffer if the myth of the "Orgy of Capri", so profitable to the tourist trade, were destroyed, the Commune managed to stifle the affair of the memorial stone in red tape; and the stone itself eventually found a more practical use—back to front—as part of the building materials used in the reconstruction of the Town Hall.

Even if modern literature on the rehabilitation of Tiberius is dull to the point of boredom, there is still some amusement to be derived from Suetonius' stories of the Emperor's life on Capri.

He had only been there a few days—his historian states—and had remained, quaking with fear, in his rocky and supposedly inaccessible dwelling, when a fisherman, hoping to win his favour, clambered up the cliff with a basket full of the fruits of his labour, and offered the Emperor a superb red mullet—"a Barble of an extraordinary bignesse", as Philemon Holland, Suetonius' Elizabethan translator, puts it. Tiberius, scared out of his wits and indignant at such temerity, ordered as a punishment that the foolhardy fisherman should have his face rubbed with the fish he had offered the Emperor. "And when the poor fellow", Suetonius continues, "amid this punishment seemed to rejoice yet, and said, It was happy that he had not offred him a Lopstar also (which he had caught) of a huge greatnesse, hee commaunded that his face should be grated and mangled likewise with the said Lopstar".

Another passage in Suetonius records the place where Tiberius "caused condemned persons after long and exquisite torments to be flung headlong before his face into the sea; where were readie to receive them a number of mariners, who with their spirits, poles and oars should beat and batt their carkasses: to the end that none of them might have any breath or wind remaining in the bodie". This story created the legend, and the local industry, of the "Leap of Tiberius". It was on the presumed site of these iniquities that the famous "Bella Carmelina" used to dance the equally famous Tarantella, and tell the true story—as true as those of Suetonius, anyway—of the great men of ancient Rome who had been thrown into the sea at Capri, beginning with Sejanus, Tiberius' Minister.

After the slanderous tales of the classical rhetoricians and the impassioned eulogies of his recent rehabilitators, history has by now struck a just balance with regard to Tiberius. After his retirement to Capri, the figure of the Emperor is enriched and completed by the figure of the man. Against the background of the island which he had made the centre of the Roman world, he appears as he really was, the First Citizen of the Republic which had become an Empire, the *Princeps civitatis*, a human figure, not a cardboard one; a man who may perhaps have known all the vices, but who did not lay false claim to any of the virtues of his age.

Ordained priest at the age of twenty, and Pontifex Maximus at a little over forty, Tiberius had had to occupy himself from the time of his youth with religious problems. At Rhodes he had followed the courses in astrology and magic, the foundations of theology. In the solitude of Capri, Tiberius had time to meditate upon the spiritual problems of the Empire, which the religious reforms of Augustus had not succeeded in solving. One of the first things to strike him must have been the inadequacy to contemporary needs of the polytheistic structure of the Roman state.

The cult of the One God, Mithras, had been introduced from the East by Tiberius' legionaries, and there were temples to Mithras on Capri. One of these stood on the site of the ancient Greek settlement, and its ruins were later used to adorn the small and ancient cathedral of San Costanzo, where was found the famous Mithraic bas-relief now in the Museum of Naples. There was another rock temple in the grotto of Matermania; and the name of this valley, derived from *Mater Magna*, the Great Mother, associates it with Cybele, the Earth Goddess, whose cult was always closely connected with that of Mithras, the Sun God. It was in this grotto that the altar mentioned by Hadrawa in his *Ragguagli*, and subsequently acquired by the British Museum, was found. An even more convincing piece of evidence of the worship of Mithras at Capri in the time of Tiberius is provided by some lines of the poet Statius, which refer to "green hills" on Capri called *Taurabulae*. These can be identified even today with the Tuoro Grande and the Tuoro Piccolo, on either side of the vale of Matermania; and their names are a reminder of the religious ceremony called the *taurobolium*, which took place in the grotto there in honour of Mithras, and which culminated in the sacrifice of a bull, as shown in the famous bas-relief in the Museum of Naples.

There is evidence that the cult of Mithras was known throughout the whole Empire. Though admitting a trinity of persons, the cult recognised a single God, as enunciated in the basic dogma: "The Sun is God, the Sky is God and the Holy Spirit (*Corax*, the black bird, a symbol of purity) is God; yet these are not three gods, but only one God: Mithras...".

While the ageing Tiberius was perhaps pondering religious reforms at Capri an event took place in the East, the importance of which he could not judge. News reached him from Pontius Pilate that one Jesus Christ, who called himself King of the Jews, had been crucified in Jerusalem.

When he was seventy-seven Tiberius, though aged and infirm, felt a desire to pay a visit to Antonia, the elderly and noble widow of his brother Drusus, in her villa at Frascati. On his way back to Capri he decided, on an impulse, to join in a boar hunt on the Promontorio Circeo. But he allowed himself to overdo things, and caught a chill. When he reached the villa of Lucullus, on Cape Misenum, he became seriously ill, and there Caligula, hastening the course of nature, piled cushions on the dying Emperor's face and smothered him.

While, in Tacitus' phrase, "the strength of Tiberius was ebbing away, but not his deceitfulness", events were also happening on Capri. To put the final touches to this picture of wickedness receiving its just reward, nature, violating her own geological laws, produced the one and only earthquake to which the island can lay claim, completing thereby the destruction of the lighthouse, which had been struck by lightning in a storm some years before. This lighthouse was the pride of Capri, and its beams had been said by Statius to rival those of the moon. Superstitious minds saw in its destruction an evil omen—the prelude to the collapse of the Roman Empire.

Historians say that out of hatred for Tiberius the Romans came to Capri after his death and destroyed all the buildings associated with him. This is probably untrue; but if the Romans did not do it, the islanders certainly did, and eighteen centuries later the remains of Roman majesty and power on Capri amply justified Gregorovius' phrase—*ein Bild wilder Verwüstung*—a picture of wild destruction.

Caligula had stayed for long periods at the court of Tiberius on Capri, and it was there that he had undergone the ritual shaving associated with the assumption of the *toga virilis* and the reaching of manhood; but once he had become Emperor he never returned to the island. If we are to believe his historians, he was too busy carrying out his mad schemes elsewhere—at Baiae, for example, where he built the famous bridge of boats which ruined the Imperial finances—or persecuting Seneca, the great moralist.

Claudius, who succeeded Caligula in A.D. 41, did not know Capri at all, and Nero, the last of the Julio-Claudian line, who ruled from 54 to 68, made Naples the scene of his follies.

Thus the great days which had brought glory and renown to the island came to an end in the first century A.D., and the story of Imperial Capri was over.

TIBÈRE.

Chapter III

THE BISHOPRIC OF THE QUAILS

After the death of Tiberius the mists of history close once more around Capri, and the island enters upon a long period of obscurity, from which historians, for all their efforts, are powerless to release it. From time to time, however, there are a few gleams of light.

The most striking event in the religious history of the island is the coming, apparently from the East, in about the sixth century, of its future patron saint, the holy Costanzo. In the ninth century the island was given its own diocese, and a small cathedral was built on the site of Costanzo's tomb, in the region of Aiano di Sotto, near the old Greek settlement. It was this church which, as mentioned in the previous chapter, was adorned with marbles from a Mithraic temple that had existed on the same spot.

The eighth century is generally taken to mark the beginning of the raids of the Barbary pirates, who had a naval base, and what one might almost call a centre of their maritime empire, at Agropolis, not far from Paestum. The gift of the island to Amalfi by the Emperor Ludwig II in the ninth century, started a connection between the island and the duchy of Naples, which had an important result. Many estates were colonised by rich landowners from the mainland, and contact with the people of Naples introduced to the island the arts and industries of the sea. Thanks to them there grew up on Capri a race of seafarers engaged in coastwise trade—shipowners and master-mariners, hardy sailors and skilled shipwrights and boatbuilders, who lived for the most part in the village of Anacapri. From Amalfi, too, first came the gifted mastermasons responsible for the local style of building, seen at its best in the Certosa di San Giacomo, the Charterhouse of Capri, and in other buildings of the Angevin period. From this style there later arose a type of domestic architecture characterised by the use of vaulted roofs, a feature found in many parts of the surrounding region, but which on Capri reached its highest stage of development.

The plague which was endemic in Italy throughout the Middle Ages and which took such toll of the population, broke out in Capri in 1493. But apart from this, very little of any wide historical significance occurred in the island during these centuries. However, the two inhabited localities, the *università*, or municipalities of the *Città* of Capri and the *Terra* of Anacapri, make up for this deficiency with the story of their internal relations, which is recorded in the documents of the diocesan and legal archives, and above all revealed in the endless cases heard before the Neapolitan criminal court, the *Summaria*.

The most celebrated of these began in 1494 and continued for three centuries. It concerned the *Porta de la diferencia*, the "Gate of Contention"—that is, the gate into the *Terra* of Anacapri. During the plague of the preceding year the gate had been torn down and thrown over the nearby precipice of Porcello by the inhabitants of Capri, who carried the bodies of victims of the plague to the upper part of the island, and thus spread the disease to the upper town. In retaliation the people of Anacapri "used to throw stones at the most holy Cross of Our Lord Jesus Christ", which the men from the lower town were in the habit of carrying in procession up to the borders of the two territories. The records of this case reveal, with a wealth of precise and circumstantial evidence, that it was no rare occurrence for the inhabitants of Capri to invade the upper territory, set fire to the houses, put some of the villagers to the sword, and force the rest to flee for their lives to Massa or Sorrento. Small wonder that one of the first recorded pronouncements by a foreigner on the inhabitants of the two villages is "...*les peuples de ces deus terres se haissent extremement*"—"the people of these two districts hate each other like poison"! From another document of the period we learn that "in the time of Duke John, the people of Capri were in revolt against the house of Aragon", and all because Frederick II of Aragon had granted equal rights to the inhabitants of Anacapri!

At the beginning of the sixteenth century the ancient kingdom of Naples, of which Capri was a part, fell into the hands of the Spaniards. A viceroy was installed in the capital, and Capri naturally shared the fortunes of the province as a whole. The island was ruled by a Governor or *Capitanio*, usually a soldier or lawyer, whose jurisdiction covered the *Città* of Capri, with its wall and castle, and the unwalled *Terra* of Anacapri (Crape and Anna-Crape in the dialect of the time), and extended to their respective Mayors and Councils. Alongside the civil power, or perhaps more accurately in opposition to it, stood the Bishop, who, as head of the diocese, exercised a theoretical control over the spiritual side of island life, and also possessed some measure of temporal power through his ecclesiastical court of justice, the Curia, and its various executive organs.

This was the sort of situation which in this same epoch brought about the struggle between Church and State. On Capri the struggle was complicated by the fact that the Carthusians, with their great monastery and rich possessions, not to mention the innumerable privileges conferred on them by a succession of Angevin and Aragonese kings, wanted to play a part in the affairs of the island.

With the coming of the Spaniards to the south of Italy in the sixteenth century there was a renewal of the raids of the Barbary pirates. In 1534 the famous pirate admiral, Kheir Eddin, known throughout the Mediterranean as Barbarossa, landed on the island and destroyed the castle of Anacapri. Twenty years later there was another raid on Capri, which did a great deal of damage, particularly to the Certosa, which was sacked. Other less damaging raids followed, and thenceforward the island lived in continual terror of the Turkish pirates, in the local idiom *con la paura dei Turchi*. Numerous references to these raiders are found in the letters, *ad limina Apostolorum*, which the Bishop wrote each year to the Holy See on the state of his diocese. One of these, written at the beginning of the seventeenth century by Monsignor Bozzuto, opens with the words, "The town and island of Capri is twenty miles distant from Naples, and is in the midst of the ocean, which is in grave danger of the Turk".

It is impossible to imagine how anyone, in the sixteenth century, could have thought the island an attractive place for a holiday. Yet this is the period that sees the growth of a flourishing literature on the history and topography of Capri, mainly in the form of "reports". The most notable of these early accounts is to be found in the *Historia Neapolitana*, a manuscript work by the great humanist Fabio Giordano, who lived in the second half of the sixteenth century. It was much praised at the time, and later by Mommsen and Beloch. It was used as a source both by historians and antiquarians in their learned guidebooks and vade-mecums for tourists, such as Cesare Capaccio's *Neapolitanae historiae*, published in 1607. Giordano's account comprises a learned dissertation, *De Capreis Insula*, and also a rough sketch map of the island, which is probably the earliest document concerning the topography of Capri.

English travellers now began to prolong the Grand Tour beyond Rome, and their literature of travel was enriched by the appearance of the *Introduction of Knowledge* by Andrew Boorde, and *Instructions for Foreign Travel* by James Howell. The first foreigner to mention Capri in his writings was George Sandys, scholar and poet, who in 1610 undertook a journey to Turkey, Egypt and the Holy Land, and to the "remote parts of Italy and Islands adjoining". One of these islands was Capri, and in his book Sandys has left us a description of the Grotta Oscura, based on that of Capaccio.

In the time of Sandys, Capri was the poorest diocese of the Roman Church; and we have only to read one of the many reports of its Bishops to the Pope, for example, that of Monsignor Raffaele Rastelli in 1632, to have some idea of its wretched condition. Bishop Rastelli was by way of being a "man of letters". He had to his credit several works on theology, to say nothing of a *Brevis Censurarum in genere Tractatus*, and was engaged on a volume dealing with the famous miracle of San Gennaro, the patron saint of Naples—which, however, he never completed.

His letter to the Pope is one long tale of woe. Right at the beginning, he points out that the income of the episcopal household, derived mainly from a tithe on quails, is approximately 160 ducats a year, "and even this", he goes on, "I have difficulty in obtaining, because people are so poor". With this sum he had to maintain two cathedral churches, San Costanzo and Santo Stefano, and provide for the needs of numerous clerics, who, contrary to custom, retained three or four livings for their own use.

The theme of his extreme poverty occurs again and again in the report, each time in more pathetic tones; and the Bishop's pleas for help get more and more desperate, until they culminate in the request that the Sacred Congregation of the Council "should deign to command that the See of Capri be united to that of Massa... for it is impossible for us to maintain ourselves on our own, owing to the headstrong nature of the islanders, and the poverty of the said See, which is brought about by these same islanders, as the poverty of the Pope is procured by the heretics...".

Here we have another motif which recurs in practically all the seventeenth-century reports *ad limina Apostolorum*: the unruliness of the inhabitants. "They steal from the Governor, the Bishop, the King and the Church!" exclaims the poor Bishop of Capri.

The good Bishop's *cri de coeur* also provides us with other pieces of information, some curious and useful, others amazing or incredible. In the island of Capri there were, according to his account, about two thousand souls. If we are to believe the Bishop, this flock consisted almost entirely of black sheep; yet to provide for its spiritual needs there existed no less than seventy churches and chapels, counting shrines, hermitages and private oratories. That at least is the figure given by a French traveller, who got his information from the Bishop's Vicar, De Curtis. The reason the Vicar gave for this state of affairs is interesting: "...*ce grand nombre d'Eglises avoit ésté fait du temps des François, affinque les femmes peusent ouir la messe sans seslogner et s'exposer a l'insolence et a l'impudicité de la nation*"— that is, of the French soldiers. Other chroniclers give a similar reason for the large number of churches and chapels in Naples in the time of the Angevins.

The Bishop's clergy were poor, undisciplined and rebellious. Monsignor Rastelli informed the Pope of the case of a canon who was being reprimanded for his loose living, when he suddenly went for the Vicar and tried to hit him. On being excommunicated for this misdemeanour he appealed to the Archbishop of Sorrento, and in the presence of witnesses asserted that for the like reason he would have attacked the Bishop, the Cardinal or even the Pope himself. By authority of the Archbishop of Naples the canon was put in jail and given into the keeping of the Vicar of Capri and two priests; but he got away in the end, because the latter were frightened of him and let him escape.

On top of these and many other afflictions there were always the Carthusians, who claimed to be outside the jurisdiction of the Bishop, and who forbade the islanders to sell the produce of their lands so that they themselves would have a good market for their own crops. When threatened with censure, they would appeal to the Viceroy, and the latter, glad to be able to assert the supremacy of the civil power, would on behalf of his protégés hurl at the unfortunate Bishop one of his "hortatory" letters, commanding him to leave the Carthusians alone. These "hortatory" letters sent by the Viceroy began, as was the Spanish custom, with many professions of respect and devotion, but soon passed on to a statement in unequivocal terms of the wishes of His Excellency, usually a Grandee of Spain, and concluded with a varied selection of insults and a series of awful threats.

The Archives of the Sacred Congregation of the Council in the Vatican contain the reports to the Holy See of many other Bishops of Capri, and they are all alike—variations, in pathetic keys, on a few recurring themes: the poverty of the diocese, the wickedness of the islanders, the dissoluteness of the clergy, the ingratitude of the Carthusians, the arrogance of the civil power, and the tyranny of the Viceroy.

Taken as a whole, these humble documents cast a vivid light on Capri's institutions and way of life, an existence typical of small communities in the south of Italy under the rule of the Spaniards, with few gleams of happiness, and many dark periods of suffering. They record the few hopes and the many anxieties, the occasional virtues, and the numerous vices of a community oppressed by foreign domination and burdened by the privileges of the monks. To quote the words of a Bishop writing to the Viceroy in 1664, the island's only source of comfort "is the grace of Our Lord Jesus Christ who causes to descend upon Capri so large a multitude of quails".

As has been said, the Bishop was dependent for his upkeep upon these birds. The French traveller whom we have already mentioned remarks that, if they pass in great numbers, "*l'evesque fera bonne chere*"; if, on the other hand, the wind makes them take another route, or if their numbers are small, "*...son revenu sera limité a 100 ou a 200 escus*" [1].

Only one of the Bishops who governed the diocese of Capri was a native of the island. This was Monsignor Mazzola, who ruled the See in the sixteenth century. Mazzola always claimed that he came from a noble family, and wishing to preserve for ever the memory of his house and of the episcopal dignity to which he himself had attained, he planned to build a lordly tomb surmounted by a tablet recording the glories of his family, the excellence of his administration and the amenities of his native isle. But alas for the hopes of mortal men! his earthly remains found a very different resting place from that which he had intended: the terrible *fossa carnaria*, or common ossuary, which bore over its entrance

---

[1] While on the subject of quails, Norman Douglas used to wonder who was the author of a curious recipe for "quail sauce", quoted by Fabio Giordano in his description of Capri: "*Finduntur a superiori parte adunato adipe reliquum corpus sale condiunt adipem liquant servantque in alabastris condientis epulis iucundissimum quod genus antiqui ignorarunt*". This recipe is given by Niccolò Perotto, Bishop of Siponto, in *Cornucopiae seu latinae linguae commentarii*, published in Paris in 1528.

the inscription: "This is the way of all flesh!". When, in the nineteenth century this vault was emptied of its macabre contents, and turned into a row of business premises, two pieces of stone, which had formed part of the projected tomb of the Bishop, came to light, each inscribed with a phrase of his epitaph.

In the spring of 1932 it was discovered that a large and almost undecipherable manuscript in the library of the École des Beaux-Arts in Paris contained an account of a journey to Capri undertaken exactly three centuries before, in May 1632. The Marquis de Chennevière, who bought the precious manuscript from a second-hand bookshop in 1850, noted that the name Bouchard, which appears in the manuscript along with those of former owners, might well be that of the author; and so it has proved. This Bouchard has now been identified as Jean-Jacques Bouchard, a gentleman of the suite of M. de Chalois. Bouchard refers to himself throughout under the Greek pseudonym of Orestes, and shows himself to be a man of learning and experience, versed in Greek, Latin and politics, an adventurer with few scruples, a lover of pleasures, a connoisseur of music, and, as he himself liked to think, a devotee of *belles-lettres*. The manuscript shows that this adventurous traveller was also an antiquarian and a numismatist. He undertook his journey to Italy provided with letters of introduction to the great scholar, Peiresc, to Cardinal Barberini, to Lucas Holstein, and to the French Ambassador at Rome, from Gassendi, the opponent of Descartes and friend of Campanella.

The first account of the island of Capri, the dissertation of Fabio Giordano, referred to above, is a magnificent piece of academic erudition, modelled on the style of Tacitus. Bouchard's account, written half a century later, is a complete contrast—a masterpiece of factual reporting, a storehouse of accurate information and of original and penetrating comments, the whole seasoned with a piquant sauce of scandal.

Bouchard had spent Shrovetide at Rome and Easter at Naples. Tiring of these pleasures he looked around him for other sources of diversion. The first thing that struck him was not the beauty of the scenery, for this is a literary invention of the nineteenth century, but the singularity of two spots in the neighbourhood, which were objects of terror for a few people, and completely ignored by everybody else: Vesuvius and Capri. The year before, on 16 December 1631, one of the worst eruptions of Vesuvius had devastated the countryside, and Bouchard decided to carry out a tour of inspection. Then someone told him about Capri, and how it lived in continual dread of the Turks. So Bouchard decided to visit the island for himself and hiring a light felucca he set out across the bay. This sail to Capri he turned to good account in an excellent topographical description of the Bay of Naples, complete with all the relevant geographical data, and enlivened by appropriate classical reminiscences.

On his arrival at Capri he put up for a couple of days at the Certosa, and visited and described all the places of interest in the island. Though his descriptions are good, the best things in his account are his comments, sometimes rather unkind, on the inhabitants, the Governor and the Bishop. However, he was grateful to the Carthusians for the hospitality they gave him: "*Orestes logea chez eus et fut magnifiquement traité: entres autres choses il mangea certaines petites ricottes...*"—a reference to the famous *ricottelle* or soft white cheeses of Capri, of which, he says, the monks "*font presents a tous les grands de Naples*". So renowned and so superb were they that it is said that when Frederick III of Naples was dispossessed of his kingdom by the French and Spanish, the Prior and some of the monks of the Certosa of Capri hurried to Ischia to present the exiled monarch with a repast of *ricottelle* and butter, in token of their sympathy.

Bouchard had little sympathy for the islanders, whom he describes as *"pauvres, orguelleus et larrons"*. He is even harder on the women: *"elles font volentier la courtoisie"*. These unfavourable comments are no exceptions among early judgments on Capri. Capaccio says that the Capresi "live in the utmost poverty but still vie with each other in pride"; a Bishop, Monsignor Bozzuto, writes that the Pope has sent him among these people as a penance for his sins; a much earlier author, Fazio degli Uberti, celebrates in verse the misdeeds of the "rash and unreliable" islanders; and Rizio calls them *fuggistenti*, idlers.

But there are topics of more importance in Bouchard's writings than his comments on the islanders. Armed with some of the major works dealing with the region, for example, Capaccio's guide-book, Ligorius' map, a description of the Kingdom of Naples by Cesare d'Engenio, and possibly the *Italia* of the famous geographer G.A. Magini, Bouchard compares and collates their accounts, and himself adds many details concerning the names of places. When he comes to make a list of Roman ruins, he adopts the local point of view which tends to see in many of them just so much old rubbish, and very sensibly refuses to accept the conventional theory of twelve villas dedicated to twelve deities, recognising only four sites as those of Imperial palaces.

From his hosts the Carthusians Bouchard learnt of their glorious history; from the Vicar he heard about all the affairs of the diocese and all the peccadillos of the clergy. In Anacapri, he visited the sacristy of the parish church and read all the local scandals of the island.

Mixed up with the local gossip of the tiny diocese are facts and events from the history of Rome, and Bouchard does not hesitate to display his classical knowledge when appropriate. His command of Greek enabled him to explain the origin of many words of the local dialect, for example *falangi*, the wooden rollers on which boats are pulled on to dry land, which Bouchard derives from the Greek *Phalanges*, "*pieces de bois sur quoy glisse le navire*".

On leaving Capri he made for Salerno, sailing along the Sorrentine peninsula from Massa to Amalfi. On the way he informed himself minutely about all the features of the Amalfi coast, and was continually taking notes, sketching and consulting maps. This behaviour finally aroused the suspicions of the sailors. Getting off at Salerno, he met with a cobbler and a surgeon who took him to a grotto. Here he found himself confronted by a captain of the Spanish army who asked him for his sword, and searched him. Finding on him a map of Capri, "*le seul plan qu'Orestes eut tracé de sa vie*", the officer put him under arrest. Bouchard had officially received the tonsure at Rome and passed for a cleric, but the letters of credit found on his person showed him to be of French nationality, and he was accordingly incarcerated in the gloomy prison of Salerno, where the head jailer, by way of consolation, said to him: "Brother, of a certainty you hang tomorrow!".

Fortunately for him the magistrate in charge of his case was a humanist, and hearing that the French adventurer was travelling out of curiosity and to improve his mind, asked him when he was brought before him for "*l'explication du premier vers du Plutus d'Aristophane*". Bouchard acquitted himself well in this test; but he did even better at Naples, where his judge, Don Juan Erasmo, Regent of the Tribunale della Vicaria, a pleasant talker, "*fort en lettres humaines*", and devoted to literature, took him under his protection, presented him with a sonnet by Marino, and set him free. In return, Bouchard dedicated a fulsome sonnet to him, and wrote another for the Viceroy, the Count of Monterey, in which he declared that he

46

would willingly remain a prisoner in "*Naples ou la prison est si douce et benigne*".

On this gay and poetic note, the French humanist and adventurer brings the account of his voyage to Capri to a close.

The Carthusian monastery (drawing by Giovan Battista Ceas - 1930)

CHAPTER IV

BAROQUE

The Baroque style in art and architecture had reached the height of its development by the middle of the seventeenth century. In France it was personified in a king, Louis XIV, who was both its culminating point and its symbol. In Italy it reached its zenith in the Accademia dell'Arcadia, and included the outstanding names of Giambattista Marino, Claudio Monteverdi, Caravaggio and Bernini. However, poetry, music, painting, sculpture and architecture were not the only spheres in which this style flourished; nor were the main centres of intellectual life its only home. In the South, where an element of melodrama was inseparably associated with the rule of the Spaniards, not only art, but the whole of life, even in the most remote communities, was steeped in the spirit of the *barrueco*. To illustrate this point, we have only to present the three main participants in the seventeenth-century life of Capri— three celebrities who just failed to make their mark: the Duke of Marianella, who nearly became the Feudal Lord of Capri; Monsignor Paolo Pellegrino, who almost qualifies for the title of its evil spirit; and the Venerable Madre Serafina di Dio, who only just missed being its first saint.

As has already been said, in Imperial times, Capri had been part of the private estate of the Caesars, and in the centuries between the collapse of the Empire and

49

the establishment of Spanish rule, its history was one long struggle to claim for itself the privileged position of *città regia*, or royal city, belonging directly to the King and not to any of his feudatories. This sometimes called for heroic measures, but Capri succeeded in resisting all attempts at feudal domination.

Because of its Imperial origins, the island was said to have been inherited by Tertullus, the descendant of the Caesars, who was supposed to have left it to the monks of Montecassino. But researches recently carried out in the Abbey of Montecassino have shown that if the monks ever really received this legacy, they never exercised their dominion over Capri. So the belief that it was in early days a fief is shown to be wrong. A second claim was associated with the name of Eliseo Arcucci, a native of Capri and Admiral of Frederick II, who was said to have been the first of a line of "Counts of Capri". This story has now been shown to be a falsification, dating from the early years of the seventeenth century, and based on a forged inscription on the tombstone of another Arcucci, Giacomo, which described the family as *Caprearum Insulae Comites*. Giacomo, Grand Chamberlain to Queen Joanna of Naples, and Count of Minervino, had many connections with Capri. He founded the Certosa and built for his royal mistress the ancient house called the "Palace" of Capri, but he was never "Count" of the island, for the simple reason that the title did not exist.

From these claims of non-existent feudal rights we pass on to other equally uncertain tenures of the island by private individuals or nobles. In 1284 it belonged to a certain Filippella, daughter of Nicola de Littera, who gave it to Charles II of Anjou; in 1311 its owner was Tommaso da Procida; later in the century its possession was unsuccessfully sought by Butillo Prignano, nephew of Pope Urban VI. By a diploma of Queen Joanna I, dated 1371, and a Bull of Gregory XI of 1375, the

Carthusians became legal owners of the most fruitful estates on the island, but this did not make them its feudal owners. Finally, in 1381 Charles III of Anjou undertook to maintain Capri and the Duchy of Amalfi as part of the Royal Demesne.

It was the boast of Capri, then, never to have been made a fief, and, in her grievous poverty, she took pride in remaining part of the royal estates. But towards the middle of the seventeenth century, an unexpected event set the island in an uproar.

During the frequent wars of that time the royal treasury was often in urgent need of money, and the king of Spain was in the habit of meeting the demands on the Exchequer by selling to rich and ambitious nobles the finest lands of his private estate. Such a fate was in store for Capri. On the occasion of the census, or "counting of hearths" in August 1643, there arrived on the island Don Antonio Barile, Duke of Marianella, bringing with him, by order of the Viceroy, a company of soldiers who were to be maintained by the municipalities of Capri and Anacapri. During his stay, he became very attached to Capri, and bought, or perhaps rebuilt, the small *palazzo* bearing his name which faces the church of Santo Stefano, and which is now part of the Palazzo Cerio.

Negotiations for the purchase of the island must have already been under way when he arrived there, and, according to documents recently discovered, Capri finally passed into the possession of Marianella for 26,000 ducats.

The islanders, as headstrong and as wilful as ever, rose up *en masse* against this attempt to reduce their island to a fief, and this time, like good parishioners, gathered around their parish priest, Don Marcello Strina, a figure of the first importance in this century, whom we will meet again as the counsellor and patron of Madre Serafina. In the *Life* of Madre Serafina by her

51

panegyrist Padre Nicolò Squillante, published in 1732, there is an account of the work of this zealous and heroic parish priest. Defying the wrath of the Viceroy and triumphing over the intrigues of the Collateral Council, he reasserted the ancient privilege of Capri never to be sold, alienated from the Royal Demesne, or reduced to vassalage, and succeeded in having Philip IV's sale of the island to the Duke of Marianella declared invalid.

But the Duke was not prepared to let matters rest here, and set in motion the whole slow, unwieldy mechanism of Hispano-Neapolitan justice, a formidable combination of procrastination and inertia. Since the King's grant of the fief had not been implemented in fact, the Duke persuaded the Viceroy, the Admiral of Castille, to confer on him the high-sounding titles of "Prince of Capri", and "Captain Perpetual of War", with an extension of his hypothetical right to Capri to include the Galli islands of the Sorrentine peninsula; and his privileges were increased by certain coveted fiscal rights: the *scannaggio dei porci* (a tax on the slaughter of pigs), the *portolanìa* (harbour dues), the *mastrodattìa* (a stamp duty on legal documents), the *pecunia maris* (a tax on fishing) together with the sole right to fish "those seas containing garfish", the most common of all the fish in the Mediterranean.

At this the two communities of Capri and Anacapri, possibly for the first time in their history, and certainly for the last, found themselves in agreement. Appealing to the Collateral Council, they demanded the intervention of the Visitor General, the Regent of the Royal Council, and even of the Viceroy himself; and in the presence of all these dignitaries, produced their trump card—a privilege signed by an ancestor of Philip IV and full of high-sounding legal terms, in which the King solemnly pledged that "*dicha Isla de Capri no se pueda jamás ensajenar ni desmembrar de mi Real*

Corona"— "the said Island of Capri shall never be severed or dismembered from my Royal Crown"!

Once again Capri had triumphed, this time against the Viceroy himself. But in 1647 the Admiral of Castille left Naples and was succeeded by the Duke of Arcos, who had not been present when the privilege had been read, and was therefore under less of an obligation to respect that awkward *jamás*. In the meantime, too, the Duke of Marianella had made other payments to the Royal Treasury, bringing the total he had contributed to date for the island of Capri to 42,000 ducats. The result was that on 25 June, the Duke of Arcos, acting on orders from Madrid, recommended the Collateral Council to grant Marianella the much desired authorisation. But this merely provoked more protests from the people of Capri, and further dithering on the part of the Supreme Collateral Council.

Marianella still continued to pour money into the Royal Treasury (the total was now 50,000 ducats), and by Royal Warrant dated from Saragossa, 28 August 1649, he was admitted to the order of the Knights of Calatrava. Meanwhile, still more ducats went in legal expenses and in attempts to win over the members of the Collateral Council. As a consolation, the Viceroy, on returning to Madrid, gave him his word that he would soon obtain the King's *exequatur*.

Fortunately for Capri, both the King and the Viceroy were Spaniards, and the Spaniards, men of their word, have one very important one, *Mañana*. And this is why the Duke of Marianella, if he were alive today, would still be waiting for his principality of Capri.

Marianella died towards the end of the century in a blaze of glory, literary glory, emanating from the most Baroque book of the seventeenth century, *Il Genio Bellicoso di Napoli*, by a longwinded Dominican panegyrist, Padre R.M. Filamondo. This volume bears the subtitle "Historical Memoirs of some celebrated Neapolitan Captains".

The judgments of the best-known and most serious diarists of the time—for example, Francesco d'Andrea in his *Avvertimenti ai nipoti* and Bucca in the *Aggionta ai Diurnali di Scipione Guerra*—are unanimously unfavourable to Marianella. The only comment of the celebrated Innocenzo Fuidoro concerns the military career of the Duke, who, he says, "did not once see service as a soldier, for, on his arrival in Milan, he was forthwith relieved of his post of Quartermaster by the Governor of that city". But Marianella's attempts to obtain the principality of Capri plus the accompanying title of "Captain Perpetual of War" were enough for Filamondo, who duly found him a place in the *Genio Bellicoso di Napoli*. And here we find his praises sung for all the deeds he would have done if he had ever succeeded in being Prince of Capri, while the portrait in words is completed by an engraving showing him in cuirass and lace, surrounded by all armoury of weapons and backed by a row of martial flags.

In 1641 Pope Urban VIII nominated as Bishop of Capri Monsignor Paolo Pellegrino, of Naples, a doctor of civil and canon law and a professor of theology. His episcopate, which lasted until 1683, was the longest and the most tempestuous in the history of Capri, and the dramatic incidents, exciting disputes and extraordinary happenings with which it abounds are of such interest that they bring to life a whole period of history.

During his tenure of the See Bishop Pellegrino tried to struggle against the royal power, get the better of the rich and powerful Carthusians, tame the rebellious citizens, reform the clergy's way of life, stop anyone (even the ecclesiastical authorities) from interfering in the affairs of his diocese, and hold in check the religious effervescence of Madre Serafina, a person even more extraordinary than he, who set out on a headlong pursuit of sanctity and very nearly attained her goal.

I have told the story of this fascinating Bishop in

detail in my book *Capri nel Seicento*. Here I can only give a brief sketch of his life and character. My account is based on the most reliable sources available: on the "hortatory" letters of the Viceroys, on Pellegrino's own reports *ad limina Apostolorum*, on reports of legal cases and other unpublished documents in the Archives of the Vatican, of the chapter and diocese of Capri, Sorrento and Amalfi, and in the State Archives of Naples, and on other documents now in the library of the Centro Caprese.

The first act in the episcopate of Monsignor Pellegrino was a general visitation of the diocese. This revealed a state of unbelievable disorder in the affairs of his See, and led to the summoning of a Synod. In convening this Synod the Bishop hoped to bring his chancellery to heel, discipline his clergy, improve their way of life and reassert the rights and privileges of the Church. By doing this he succeeded in raising a hornet's nest. A constant maxim of previous bishops had been to leave well alone; Pellegrino's motto was to revolutionise. In July 1642, as soon as the results of the Synod were published, he began systematically to put its recommendations into practice. He demanded the return of all Church property, and required the holders of benefices to submit themselves to the judgment of the Ecclesiastical Court, threatening with censure and excommunication all those who refused.

The islanders, alarmed, appealed for help to the Viceroy, who sent the Bishop a "hortatory" letter urging him, "as becometh a good prelate", to revoke the edicts of the Synod, which, he declared, "were null and void, and harmful to the jurisdiction of the King".

The Bishop thereupon appealed to the Pope, denouncing the persecutions of the Viceroy, for the Viceroy as a punishment had already imprisoned one of the Bishop's brothers. But the Pope was unmoved, and Monsignor Pellegrino had to return to the attack himself with new threats and menaces. Further "hortatory" letters showered on Capri, each more threatening than the last. The Bishop excommunicated the rebellious citizens, who, in order to escape damnation, were forced to pay an indemnity in candles to the Church. Reviewing the Bishop's activities, the Viceroy called him unfitted for his ministry and reminded him that it was abhorrent to the Sacred Canons of the Church to demand money for the administering of absolution, as Monsignor Pellegrino had been doing. Even the Metropolitan Archbishop of Amalfi was shocked, and sent a notary, Filippo Viva, to present to the Bishop of Capri an act of reprobation from the Ecclesiastical Court of Amalfi. But the Bishop got his nephew and some other clerics to give the notary a "solemn thrashing", and the emissary of the Archbishop of Amalfi left the island in a somewhat worse condition than that in which he had come.

But these were only preliminary skirmishes in the war which was soon to break out between Capri and the great hostile powers, the Archbishoprics of Amalfi and Sorrento, and the Viceroy at Naples. Fortunately war with the "foreigner" was interrupted by the struggle between the Bishop and his own clergy. The twelfth chapter of the Synod, *De vita et honestate clericorum*, had just been published, and Bishop Pellegrino was determined to enforce it. This chapter prescribed, among other things, that priests were to wear their cassocks "fastened at the neck, so that in no wise should the chest appear uncovered". Coloured shoes and fancy laces were prohibited. Only doctors and other dignitaries might wear a ring, and then only a simple one. In addition, all clerics were forbidden to hunt or fish: "let them rather, by their good example, make themselves fishers of souls". They were not allowed to go swimming in the sea in public, but only in private, and suitably clad with due propriety. They were not to frequent shops, which in this island, the Synod said, were more like taverns. And lastly, they were not to be seen about in the company of women.

All this happened in the first years of his episcopacy, but it was nothing compared with what was to come.

So far the Bishop had made but gentle use only of his power of excommunication, a power which terrified alike rich and poor. Now, since he had his own law-courts and his own prison, and no longer trusted in the obedience of his clergy, he set up a body of armed guards formed from the ushers of his court. By day they maintained order in the country, but at night they roamed about, drinking and rioting and beating up all who were in disagreement with their Bishop. The people of the island caed them the *Percussori*.

The Viceroy demanded the punishment of these guards for their scandalous nocturnal behaviour, and sent the Recorder of the Royal Court to Capri to insist upon their imprisonment. The Bishop's reply was to excommunicate the sailors whose boat had brought the royal official to the island. So in order to strengthen the civil power and keep the Bishop in check, the Viceroy nominated as Governor of Capri a Spaniard, Don Honofreo Sanchez, Grandee of Spain. Out of this act there grew a serious conflict concerning etiquette and prerogative. Grandees of Spain have the right to remain covered even before the King; and the Viceroy of Naples, who represented the King, ranked as a *grandissimo* of Spain, and had, theoretically at least, the right never to take off his hat to anyone, not even to God. As a result of the intolerance of the Bishop of Capri, before many days were out, a conflict arose between the Bishop and Don Honofreo Sanchez, in which these complicated prerogatives were pushed to the extreme limits of their application.

In their possessions in Italy the Spaniards had

made it a rule that at solemn religious functions senior royal officials—that meant at Capri the Captain Governor—should sit on a seat less ornate than that of the Bishop, but no farther away from the High Altar. Now it happened that when Don Honofreo called for the first time on the Bishop to pay his respects as a Grandee of Spain he kept on his hat. To punish him for this slight, on Palm Sunday Monsignor Pellegrino ordered the Governor's chair and the bench on which the King's men sat to be moved back from their accustomed places. During the service Don Honofreo had to suffer this affront; but on entering the church on Maundy Thursday he got his men to move both chair and bench back to their place beside the Bishop's throne. At this, as one account has it, the Bishop "exclaimed with a loud voice: 'Who the devil has moved this chair here?'" and seizing it with his hands overturned it on the Altar steps, while the Blessed Sacrament was exposed and the Canons were celebrating the sacred office. During the commotion which followed the Governor left.

For the last two days of Holy Week there was peace on the island. But on Holy Saturday Don Honofreo Sanchez, Governor of Capri, Knight of the Sword and Cape, Grandee of Spain and representative of His Excellency the Viceroy, while assisting, humbly and with bared head, at the solemn religious ceremonies, suddenly remembered his prerogatives, and since the Blessed Sacrament represented God, and he, Don Honofreo, represented the Viceroy, he clapped on his head his large plumed hat, and so proclaimed his defiance of the Bishop.

Unprecedented scandal. Warrants of excommunication for the Governor. Intervention of the Viceroy, with new and furious "hortatory" letters, calling Monsignor Pellegrino a lackey, a boor, a *picaro* and worse. Excommunication of the Viceroy. Intervention of the

Metropolitan, Monsignor Stefano Quaranta, Archbishop of Amalfi. Excommunication of the Metropolitan, "not as Archbishop but as guilty of error". In his own diocese, maintained Monsignor Pellegrino, the occupant of an see can excommunicate any other Bishop, even the Pope, who is Bishop of Rome. But fortunately things did not come to this pass, for the Pope remained silent and did not bother himself about the diocese of Capri—the Spaniards of Naples, anyway, had done little to earn his approval.

In the meantime a band of armed men sent by the Archbishop of Amalfi landed on Capri. The bells rang out the alarm, but the people of Capri seemed unwilling to help their pastor, and the invaders, *cum magno terrore totius insulae*, called upon the Bishop and his bodyguard of clergy to lay down their arms. The Bishop's reply was to place the island under a general interdict, for it had been contaminated by the "foreign" troops of the Metropolitan. Churches were shut, religious ceremonies suspended, the sacraments, even Baptism and Extreme Unction, were forbidden.

Smarting under the insult received *ad modum bellum* from the invasion of the twenty-five armed men from Amalfi, the Bishop complained to Rome about the behaviour of the Metropolitan; and while Rome was considering the case Monsignor Pellegrino was sent away from Capri. But peace could not last for long. The general interdict was removed and the Bishop came back; and for nearly forty more years of troubled, turbulent and contentious rule he continued to struggle against all-comers.

Hardly had he reoccupied his diocese when he fell out with the Carthusians. Strife between the Bishops of Capri and the Carthusians was an old story, for the Bishops resented the privileges which the Prior exercised as a mitred abbot. The tithe on quails gave the Bishop control of the air, but the Certosa undoubtedly had dominion over the land, with the right of free pasture for its goats and the *scannaggio dei porci*, to say nothing of the *pecunia maris*, which gave it control of the sea. However, Monsignor Pellegrino discovered a document attributing to him the *decima decimarum*, a "tithe of tithes", on all fish caught, and with this he launched his attack.

In answer, the Carthusians invoked an ancient privilege whereby no-one could bring wine into the island unless the monks had already sold all the wine in the Certosa wine-cellar; and with this they successfully prevented the Bishop importing wine from his own vineyard near Naples.

The struggle continued on various other pretexts until 1656, when plague broke out on the island. Many of the clergy working among the victims caught the pestilence and died, among them the good parish priest, Don Marcello Strina. As a result, insufficient secular priests were left to administer the sacraments to the dying, and Monsignor Pellegrino appealed to the Prior of the Carthusians, who had shut themselves up in their monastery to avoid contagion, to send monks to help in the work.

His letter to the Prior ends with the phrase: "I rely on your accustomed charity, which I am confident will wish to unite itself to that of Our Saviour, who laid down His life for us". The reply of the Prior, Padre Rosa, was evasive, but allowed it to be understood that the assistance asked of them "was an office repugnant to their vocation, for they were vowed to strict observance of the cloister". This was one of the few times in which the people of Capri were in agreement with their Bishop, and many bodies of plague victims were thrown over the walls of the Carthusian monastery.

By an ancient privilege the Carthusians were allowed to inherit the possessions of families which had become extinct. After the pestilence, which started in

June and went on for five months, causing the death of half the population of Capri, the already considerable estates of the Carthusians were swelled by the addition of many new lands.

Further disputes concerning the question of the Bishop's wines, the tithe on quails, *il pesce alla Pietra* (the Bishop's obligation to buy his fish at the little fish market of la Pietra, and not to get it direct from the sea), involved him with the Curia, the Certosa and the municipal authorities; and quarrels with his own clergy compelled him to leave the island yet again. From this enforced absence he did not return until 1672. Immediately he resumed hostilities with Madre Serafina, but her powerful protectors succeeded in having him removed for a third time.

On the death of Clement X in 1676 Monsignor Pellegrino, arguing that the *beneplacitum* which kept him away from Capri was now ineffective, returned to the island. But his persecutors managed to arrange that he should be removed once more, and at Naples in 1682 he resigned his See and died in the following year. In the words of his successor he had "borne many labours and discomforts and suffered many tribulations".

Madre Serafina, who after her death became the Venerable Serafina di Dio, was a certain Prudentia Pisa of whom we first hear at the beginning of the seventeenth century. In addition to over a thousand letters written by her to "diletto Giesù", most of which were lost at her death, much has been written and published about this unusual woman. The most important account of her life was written by her confessor, Don Lutio Clemente, the chief witness in her favour in the cause for her beatification. Her activity as an educator and organiser is described in a diary in which two of her oblates, Sister Angela Fortunata and Sister Ammirabile della Solitudine, acting on the advice of Don Ottavio Pisa, Penitentiary of the Cathedral of Naples, noted down day by day from 1666 to 1689 the main events in the life of their Superior, who during these years was head of the Convent of the Saviour founded by her at Capri.

Born at Naples in 1621 of Colantonio Pisa, a merchant, and Giustina Strina, of Capri, Prudentia was brought to Capri when she was two ears old and remained there for the rest of her life. Her panegyrists have seen in the stories of her childhood signs of a precocious sanctity. As soon as she had learnt her letters, she was given to read the *Lives of the Holy Martyrs* and at the age of seven, the *Life of Saint Teresa*. From these she learnt the spiritual advantages to be derived from self-inflicted sufferings and imitated in her own person the mortifications of Saint Teresa.

At the same age as Saint Teresa, fourteen, she succumbed to her first temptation. Following the example of other girls of her age, she was overcome by a desire to make herself up during the carnival; so she arranged her hair in plaits on either side of her face, decked herself with orange-blossom, rubbed her face with lard, to make it nice and shiny, and, thus embellished, looked at her reflection in a basin of water. Then she ran out of the house and watched the carnival revels from the arcade of the Case Grandi. But this sinful action caused her great anguish. She began to write a series of letters to the parish priest, accusing herself of unheard-of crimes.

When she was just fifteen her father found her a husband, a rich Frenchman, Simon Gil, and told her she must make up her mind to accept him within twenty-four hours. Prudentia asked to be allowed to spend these twenty-four hours with a pious counsellor, Donna Ippolita Conte, and during the night, with the complicity of this woman, she cut off her hair, put on a habit, and the following day, going to her confessor, announced that she wanted to become a nun. Prudentia's youthful revolt was much praised by her biographer, but it infuriated her father, and it was only by the intercession of her uncle Don Marcello Strina that she was allowed to return home. She was shut up in the woodshed, and had to promise to stop wearing her habit, and to let her hair grow again.

Young Prudentia, uncertain in health, tormented by self-imposed penances, and attacked on all sides by the devil, was going through the same sort of spiritual crisis which had faced Teresa of Avila a century before. Hallucinations multiplied, heavenly apparitions became a commonplace. Finally, when she was ecstatically embracing the figure of Christ Crucified, Whose holy wounds she had always revered, she heard the figure speak to her and reveal the Real Presence of Christ, a privilege which only a few saints have been vouchsafed in this life. The miraculous crucifix is still preserved in the convent which was founded at Massa Lubrense.

When Prudentia Pisa reached the age of twenty, her father allowed her to retire to a noble house in Naples, where she donned the habit of the Dominican order. In 1645 on the death of her father she made her full profession and entered a convent. Assuming the name of Suor Serafina, she came to Capri and, with the help of Don Marcello Strina, her uncle, and the support of many noble families of Naples, founded a small house of retreat for young women. In this she soon showed herself an excellent organiser, with a surprising talent for improvisation and remarkable business acumen.

After the success of the first house of retreat, she gained the support of dignitaries and prelates of the Church. She secured the financial backing of generous patrons, won the approbation of the future Pope, Cardinal Farnese, declared war on the quarrelsome Bishop of Capri and even extorted some generous offers from the Viceroy, himself no mean practitioner in the art of extortion. The result was that within a few years she was able to found two large convents on the island, at Capri and at Anacapri, and five others on the mainland. The building of these seven convents and their respective churches was the greatest achievement of this extra-ordinary woman.

When she was at the height of her power, she began to be troubled by the opposition of the Bishop's court, which claimed jurisdiction over her convent. Monsignor Pellegrino wanted her to give her oblates orthodox names, and not the fanciful, if poetic, ones they usually adopted: Emerald of Splendour, Angela of the Desert, Admirable of Solitude, Jewel of the Sky... In Rome the Sacred Office ordered that these names should be banned.

Her correspondence with the Spanish ascetic Miguel de Molinos, the founder of Quietism, was taken as proof that she inclined towards the Quietist doctrines, and when Molinos was imprisoned and condemned by the Inquisition, Madre Serafina too had to undergo a trial, as a result of which she was confined to her cell, and forced to renounce and confute the attractive but heretical doctrines of her friend.

Another trial occurred when she gave her approval to the "visions" of a certain Padre Acuzio, Vicar of Capri in 1676. Finally, there was a third and much more serious trial, begun in 1685 and reopened in 1689, in which the theological propositions contained in her writings were accused and condemned. She was once again found guilty, and confined to her cell, but the sentence was later commuted by the intercession of her protectors. These trials undermined the foundations of her work, and signs of decadence and revolt began to appear in her convents, especially in the Convent of the Saviour, of which she was the Superior.

Old, and unable to fit in with changing times, Madre Serafina became ill, so ill that the doctors were driven to prescribe the extreme remedy of a hot bath. But to no avail. She died alone on 17 March 1699. Her body was stretched out on her bed in the form of a cross, a fact which excited much comment on the island. First the nuns, then the clergy, and finally the whole population recognised in her mortal remains the signs of miraculous preservation.

The cause for the canonisation of Madre Serafina began soon after her death, and went on till 1865, but it was unsuccessful, and so she is remembered only as the Venerable Madre Serafina di Dio.

A corner of the Piazza

The Duke of Marianella, "Prince of Capri"

CHAPTER V

ROCOCO

The eighteenth century opens with the appearance
in Capri in 1701 of another English traveller and man
of letters, Joseph Addison, who describes the island in
Remarks on several parts of Italy, etc., published in London in 1705. A French translation of Addison's description appeared in the fourth volume of the *Nouveau
Voyage d'Italie* (Utrecht, 1722), and, since it was copied
by many writers, it helped to perpetuate the error made
by Addison in identifying the Sirens' rocks with the
Faraglioni. After describing the Grotta Oscura, Addison had written: "Not far from this Grotto lie the *Sirenum Scopuli*, which Virgil and Ovid mention in Aeneas'
Voyage; they are two or three sharp rocks that stand
about a stone's throw from the South of the Island".

A century later the mistake was repeated by Sir
R.C. Hoare in his *Classical tour through Italy* (London,
1819). Hoare gives a curious interpretation of the name
Tragara, which he derives from *tre are* (three altars),
and is the first to mention the abundance of partridges
in the hills of Capri ("Red-legged partridges in the Capri hills").

Capri, meanwhile, following the fortunes of the
Kingdom of Naples, was moving into a new and hap-
pier age, occasioned by the change from the Spaniards
to the Austrians, and from the Austrians to the Bourbons. In 1707 the Kingdom was occupied by Charles

VI of Austria, who was also Charles VI of Naples and IV of Sicily. A new era began in 1734, when the son of Philip V of Spain, Charles of Bourbon, ascended the throne of Naples, making it the royal seat of an independent kingdom, and Naples became once more a capital city. The partridges of which Hoare wrote at the beginning of the nineteenth century attracted the new ruler, who was a great sportsman, to Capri; and on visiting the island he saw that it was also a veritable mine of antiquarian remains. Whereupon Charles, who aspired to emulate the glory of the French kings, and to make his palace of Caserta a new Versailles, conceived the idea of adorning the palace with the pieces of marble which were lying in profusion in the ruins of the villas of Augustus and Tiberius; and he ordered the Governor of the island to prepare a report on these remains.

The Governor, Don Giuseppe Maria Secondo, seizing the opportunity of displaying his vast classical and antiquarian knowledge, produced the masterly "Historical report of the Antiquities, Ruins and Remains of Capri humbly offered to the King" (*Relazione storica dell'Antichità, Rovine e Residui di Capri umiliata al Re*, Napoli, 1750), a valuable monograph on the remains of the Augustan and Tiberian periods. It was incorporated two years later into the second volume of Gori's *Symbolae litterariae*. This report contains the first rational account of Tiberius' stay on Capri, and thus provides the starting-point for all the pro-Tiberius literature of the nineteenth century. It was Secondo, too, who noticed the presence of features characteristic of a Mithraic shrine in the Grotto of Matermania.

Unfortunately, the work of the learned Governor of Capri had two unhappy results. It caused the spoliation of the island's most important marbles, which were taken away to enrich the Palace of Caserta, and it gave Hadrawa the idea of carrying out the first excavations

68

on Capri, with devastating results to the island's already sadly depleted archaeological inheritance.

In the second half of the century Charles, with the title of Charles III, ascended the throne of Spain, and was succeeded at Naples by his son Ferdinand IV. Like his father, Ferdinand was a great sportsman, interested in quail as well as partridge, and for this reason was a frequent visitor to Capri.

But these kings, archaeologists and aristocratic travellers were only of minor importance in the history of Capri. Towards the middle of the eighteenth century, a leading character appears: Sir Nathaniel Thorold.

This extraordinary man is frequently mentioned in eighteenth and nineteenth-century literature; but until the beginning of this century he remained wrapped in the mystery with which he chose to surround himself on his arrival in Capri. To trace his origins, we must go to a small village in Lincolnshire where is preserved a genealogy of the various branches of the family, which, with the evidence afforded by several tombstones, helps to reconstruct the story of this man.

Innocent but entertaining inaccuracies among these records help to build up the true story of Sir Nathaniel's life. One of these is contained in the following note in the pedigree of the Thorolds of Harmston:

SIR NATHANIEL THOROLD, Baronet—Sir *Samuel* Thorold left his estates at Harmston to his distant cousin Nathaniel, son of John and Anne Thorold of the Grantham branch who was created a Baronet, 24 March 1740, with remainder to his distant kinsman Charles, youngest son of Sir John Thorold, who, however, died without issue.

Sir Nathaniel suffered from Asthma and being also deeply in debt quitted England in 1760 and travelled to Leghorn; where he met with a lovely girl of Capri, and was hence attracted to visit her native island, where he lived with her in a house he built of such character as to be termed " Palazzo" adorned externally with his armorial bearings, and became a collector of Greek and Roman antiquities. His eldest son, whom he sent to England, inherited his estates at Harmston at his death and his other progeny took possession of his house and property at Capri, where he was termed Natale Thorold; and until lately some relics of his property remained in that Island.

What these inaccuracies are we shall see later.

In eighteenth-and nineteenth-century literature there are various references to Thorold by visitors to Capri. He is mentioned by William Russell, the author of *Letters from a young painter abroad*, 1750, first published anonymously, and also by the celebrated astronomer La Lande, in *Voyage d'un François en Italie*, 1769. Coyer, another Frenchman, was moved to exclaim (1791): " *J'ai presque ambitionné le sort d'un voyageur anglais...* "; and in the same year Duclos (*Voyage en Italie*) wrote of him: " *Le premier meuble dont il se fournit pour adoucir sa solitude fut une jeune et belle fille...* ". Others who speak of Thorold are Hadrawa, Von Rehfues in *Gemählde von Neapel* (1808), Schöner and Sir Lees Knowles, to mention only a few.

But the most original sources of the Thorold story are to be found in contemporary documents: in reports of Bishops, scandalised by the presence of an *Anglo heterodoxo* at Capri, to say nothing of his conduct; in the parish registers of Capri, the *stati d'anime*; in chronicles and local traditions; and in the *Memorandum* of an Englishman, Doctor Clark, who came to Capri during the nineteenth century.

Some time before 1750, and not in 1760, as his pedigree says, Sir Nathaniel, up to his eyes in debt, but with a tidy sum of money in his pocket realised by the sale of part of his lands, left Lincolnshire and went to

Holland, intending to lay out his little hoard in some profitable manner. On the quayside of the port of Volendam the Protestant gentleman met and made friends with a Jew from Leghorn, a certain Almagià, who, penniless and in search of fortune, was awaiting the return of a large fishing fleet which had sailed in the spring to fish for cod on the Bacalaos bank, off Newfoundland.

A few days later, while watching the unloading of an immense catch, Almagià told Thorold of an idea he had had. This fabulous fish, which the Norwegians had been the first to catch off their own coasts, was usually slit down the middle and hung up on poles to dry in the wind. As such, it had formed for centuries the staple diet of the poor in northern countries, and particularly of the armies which ranged over the plains of North Europe—Muscovy, Poland, Germany, France, the Low Countries. Because it was hung on poles to dry it was known as stock-fish. But preserved in this manner alone, the stock-fish, the *piscis durus* of the Middle Ages, did not last in hot climates. What a fortune it would produce, what a blessing it would prove, this fish, if some way could be found of preserving it against the heat, for then it could be supplied to the vast Catholic population of the Mediterranean, forced to abstain from meat on Fridays and in the seasons prescribed by the Church.

The Anglican, having listened attentively, set his mind to work on the matter; and a few weeks later, after having some experiments carried out by a master-salter of herrings, announced to the Jew that the Catholic problem was solved, by the use of a salting technique similar to that employed in the salting of the Dogger bank herrings.

In this manner, in 1745 or 1746, at Volendam in Holland, Sir Nathaniel Thorold, Bart., invented salted cod.

The first cargo of salted codfish arrived at Leghorn in 1747, consigned to a friend of Almagià, the apothecary Antonio Canale. With it came Thorold, who without losing any time attached himself to old Canale's wife, a young and beautiful girl from Capri called Anna della Noce. According to the *Memorandum* of Dr Clark:

> Sir Nathaniel was struck by the marvellous beauty of Anna della Noce, for such was the maiden name of the Signora Canale, and at once fell desperately in love with her. He at once hired apartments in her house, paid her the greatest attention and finally won her heart. Her poor old doting husband regarded the attentions of the lodger to his wife as so many compliments paid to himself, and never ceased to boast to his friends of the disinterested kindness of the English Baronet.

But, as Clark philosophically observes, the course of true love never runs smooth, and the intimacy of Thorold and Anna aroused the envy and jealousy of rivals and scandalmongers, and provoked the indignation of the Church and its canonical sanctions. However much Don Antonio Canale, summoned by the Vicar Apostolic to *reddere rationem*, might protest the fidelity of his wife and the trustworthiness of his noble friend, the persecutions increased, and the scandal became more public, so that in the end the three of them were forced to leave Leghorn.

Thorold took advantage of this to transfer his business to Naples. In Genoa and Leghorn salted codfish had been greatly acclaimed; in Naples it enjoyed a positive triumph. However, even in the most beautiful and most unfortunate of European kingdoms, the lovers were not happy. Their persecution continued, and on the suggestion of Anna della Noce, Sir Nathaniel decided to make his home on Capri, which thus became for many years the centre of his activities, the capital of the realm of the salted cod.

Thorold's beautiful home, the Palazzo Inglese, despite its ruinous condition, is still one of the finest examples of local architecture on Capri. It was built on the foundations of a *casa palaziata* belonging to Monsignor Gallo, Bishop of Capri, at the end of the seventeenth century. The reconstructions were carried out by the famous master-mason Marziale Desiderio, who had originally been brought to Capri to build the church that was to serve as the Cathedral. Desiderio, incidentally, was the founder of the "Marzianello" family, to which the island owes many of its finest buildings. At the end of the eighteenth century the Palazzo Inglese, still sumptuously furnished, was the favourite residence of the King of Naples, who came twice a year to Capri to shoot quail. Later Hudson Lowe, Governor of the island during the English occupation and future gaoler of Napoleon on St Helena, installed himself there in great comfort; during the siege of Capri the house became the headquarters of the English troops, and was seriously damaged by fire-balls from the French cannons sited in the hermitage of Cetrella.

On Capri the idyll of Sir Nathaniel and Anna della Noce flowered once more; and its fruits were a numerous and happy progeny which delighted the old age of Don Antonio. Naturally, there was a scandal here too— but a scandal of a friendly nature and with a humorous basis, like all the scandals of Capri. The Bishop of Capri, Monsignor Rocco, in his report *ad limina Apostolorum* of 1754, informed His Holiness that "a scandal had been caused by the co-habitation, for almost ten years, of a certain married woman from outside the island with an heretical English nobleman...". The Pope must have had something else to do because he does not seem to have interfered in the affairs of Palazzo Inglese. The Bishop of Capri, however, although he detested and condemned sin, wished not the death but the repentance, and also the financial support, of the sinner; and he redoubled his efforts to lead the blackest sheep of all his undisciplined flock back into the fold.

But although he did everything in his power to bring about the conversion of Thorold, he was always prevented from finding common ground with him because of the language difficulty. In all the years of his residence in Italy, Sir Nathaniel had never learnt more than a single, but extremely useful, Italian word: *Pazienza*. Speaking of the death of Sir Nathaniel, Clark's diary says:

> When his strength began to fail, not having made any profession of faith, the Bishop of the Island and a surgeon of the British Navy resident in Capri, both friends of Thorold, did their best to persuade him to embrace the Catholic religion, but without result. When his end drew near, Anna della Noce and his friends renewed their prayers, and as his mind was wandering they thought that he was agreeing to receive the sacraments. The Bishop was summoned, and arrived in procession, followed by the Canons of the Cathedral. But to all the entreaties, requests and injunctions of the Bishop, Sir Nathaniel's only reply was "Pazienza". And he went on repeating the same word, for many hours, until death overtook him.

There was an interlude, however, in the solemn event; the exnaval surgeon, Husberth, intervened to urge the dying man to make a will, but all he could get out of Thorold was "Pazienza", and the Baronet died peacefully on 28 August 1764.

It took seven years of litigation for the complicated tangle of the Thorold inheritance to be unravelled, and then, according to Dr Clark, a ship of the Royal Navy was sent by the Lord Chancellor to bring back to England the body of the deceased baronet. But to find his body was the problem. According to the *Memorandum*:

> ...The exact site of his grave was unknown at the time, as the two men who had managed the sepulture had

74

died. After a fruitless search for the body, and being at the same time unwilling to disoblige the Keeper of the King's conscience, it was suggested to exhume the body of an hermit who resided on the side of Villa Jovis and who was interred under the cell he had so long inhabited. The suggestion was carried out, and the remains of the monk of Tiberio were transported to England and placed in a sarcophage designed by the Lincolnshire Baronet for his own resting place.

This substitution of corpses was the origin of the second mistake in the Thorold family records in Harmston, for, under the tombstone dedicated to Sir Nathaniel, lie the remains of the monk of Tiberio. This hermit succeeded the hermit Fra Gennaro Alba, of Naples, who died in 1729, and was himself succeeded by the hermit Andrea Polito, of Capri, who died in 1782, but of the man whose body was removed from its temporary resting place beneath his cell there remains not the slightest trace, either bodily or in writing! On the other hand, near the springs of Marucella, where tradition has it that the English Baronet introduced the growing of cress, *Nasturtium officinale*, sent out to him from Lincolnshire, must assuredly lie Sir Nathaniel's *disiecta membra*.

In the end Sir Nathaniel succeeded in repaying the island for the only Italian word he learnt during his long stay there, for he enriched its language with a proverbial expression which is still used by the inhabitants, though ignorant of its origin. When they want to put something off indefinitely the say in dialect, "*Baibai dicette 'u 'Nglese*". The phrase was coined by Bishop Rocco of Capri, who, preoccupied with the salvation of the soul of his friend the *Anglo heterodoxo*, tried repeatedly to convert him to the Catholic faith; and after Canale's death, left no stone unturned in his efforts to persuade him to marry Anna della Noce. But every time he visited him and urged him to regularise the relationship by getting married, Thorold, although not refusing, would procrastinate, telling him that they would speak of it later, *by and by*. And he continued to give this answer until his death, whereupon the disconsolate Monsignor Rocco was heard to sigh and murmur sadly to himself, "*Baibai disse l'Inglese*".

The end of the eighteenth century is remembered by antiquarians as the beginning of the first regular excavations on Capri. The man responsible was Norbert Hadrawa, who had really come to Capri for the quail shooting, but had also been authorised to poke around in the ruins of the Augusto-Tiberian palaces to see if he could find anything worthy of the Royal Museums at Naples. His famous letters, or, to give them their full title, *Ragguagli dei vari scavi e scoverte d'antichità fatte nell'Isola di Capri*, one of the greatest bibliographic rarities in the literature of the island, were written to tell one of his friends about these excavations. By profession an Austrian diplomat, Hadrawa was also, and above all, an astute dealer in antiquities, numbering among his best clients collectors like Sir William Hamilton, the Prince of Schwarzenberg and Styvens. Several fine pieces of the Hamilton Collection in the British Museum came from Capri, among them a veiled head of Tiberius. Other antiquities in the British Museum originating from Capri are No. 2541 of the Townley collection—a puteal or well-head decorated with figures of satyrs—several fragments of tessellated pavements, and various marbles, among them the so-called candelabrum or altar of Cybele, which is one of the most beautiful pieces of Greco-Roman sculpture in existence.

There has been a continual tendency to exaggerate the richness of the works of art which adorned the palaces of the Caesars in Capri. Among the real treasures must be mentioned the Greek sundial preserved in the Casa Mac Kowen in Anacapri, and the wonderful lachrymatory or tear-vase of oriental alabaster described by

Norman Douglas in *Some Antiquarian Notes*. This was discovered by Dr I. Cerio, and is now in the Studio of Via Tragara. In the neighbouring villa of La Certosella is the statuette of a Pharoah, an excellent piece of archaic Egyptian work found on the site of the Imperial villa at Castiglione. It is the only example of Egyptian art to have been discovered on Capri, and may have formed part of the *res vetustate et raritate notabiles* which Augustus brought back to Capri from Egypt. The famous "Vase of Monticello", which would have rivalled the Portland Vase, has unfortunately disappeared. There is finally a fragment of a glass cameo dish, picked up in the Grotta dell'Arsenale, and now in the Metropolitan Museum of New York; it was bought from a fisherman for 5 lire, and sold for 5,000 dollars.

Sir William Hamilton was a great friend of Ferdinand IV, and must certainly have come to Capri as a guest of the King, but he has left no trace of his passing on the island. But the learned nobleman, whose monumental work on the Phlegrean Fields entitles him to be called the greatest vulcanologist of his time, is known not so much for his writings and his antiquarian collections as for his having been the husband of Lady Hamilton—*Emma Liona*, as she was called at Naples. And Lady Hamilton, despite her radiant beauty, never found a place in the hearts of the Neapolitans because of her intimate friendship with the hated Queen Carolina.

As for Nelson, his glory was tarnished by the part he played in the restoration of the Bourbons, after the failure of the revolution of 1799 and the fall of the Parthenopean Republic. For the whole of the nineteenth century the name of the great English Admiral was associated in Italian minds with that of Admiral Caracciolo, one of the heroes of the revolution, who was declared a "traitor" and hanged from the yardarm of the English flagship, while the English fleet hovered menacingly off the Neapolitan coast.

The end of the century is marked by the failure of Goethe to land on Capri. The poet passed by Tiberius' rock on his way back from Sicily, but was filled with terror at the sight of the local shepherds, whose cries made even more terrifying—*um so schauerlicher*—the forbidding aspect of the island.

Capri consoled herself by giving an honoured welcome to the Marquis Donathien Alphonse de Sade, who arrived with letters of introduction from Ferdinand IV. De Sade's return for the many courtesies he received from the Governor of Capri was to make the island the setting of a scene of one of his novels, *Juliette*, in which he exalted the criminal glory of Tiberius.

The last important figure of the eighteenth century and also the last Bishop of Capri—the diocese being abolished after his episcopacy—was Monsignor Nicola Saverio Gamboni, a protégé of Pope Pius VII. An aristocrat, a reformer of manners and a supporter of new ideas and new ways, he was the most illustrious Bishop ever to have ruled the diocese of Capri. In 1786 he abolished the hated and iniquitous *pecunia maris*, which the Carthusians had levied since 1371, and founded a seminary and schools of arts and crafts. He was made an abbot and a baron by Ferdinand IV, but then fell into disgrace for his liberal ideas and was imprisoned and exiled. At Rome he made friends with Napoleon's uncle, Cardinal Flesh, and was made Bishop of Vigevano and sent to Milan as counsellor to Napoleon's Viceroy, Beauharnais. He was also a friend of Madame de Staël, and it was he who told her the story of the crowning of Corinna on the Campidoglio, which suggested to her the title of her famous novel.

His memory is preserved on Capri by a tablet on the walls of the Seminary, now one of the buildings of Palazzo Cerio.

Island of Capri (from D.A. Parrino), 1700

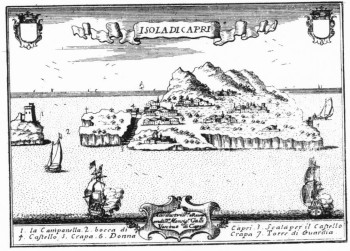

Island of Capri (from G.B. Pacichelli), 1703

CHAPTER VI

LITTLE GIBRALTAR

On the Arc de Triomphe in Paris, among the victories of Napoleon, appears the French version of the island's name, CAPRÉE, and one of the streets of the twelfth Arrondissement, near the Bois de Vincennes is also called after the island. The explanation may be in the capture of Capri, which, as we are informed by Frédéric Masson, the author of *Fastes de la Gloire*, "*...fut une des plus jolies actions de guerre de la période impériale*".

At the beginning of the nineteenth century the island formed part of the Kingdom of the Two Sicilies. Ferdinand IV ruled the Kingdom, and Maria Carolina, daughter of Maria Theresa of Austria and sister of Marie Antoinette of France, ruled Ferdinand. Ferdinand was a member of the anti-French Second Coalition, and it was not long before he had to answer for his temerity to the all-conquering armies of the new Republic. In 1798 the French armies under General Championnet, Joubert's second-in-command in Italy, swept down the peninsula, captured Rome and moved on towards Naples. The King and the court fled to Palermo, and on 23 January 1799, the Parthenopean Republic was proclaimed. However, reverses suffered by the French armies in North Italy forced Championnet's successor Macdonald, the future hero of Wagram, to evacuate the bulk of his forces from Naples. The small

81

garrison which he left behind was soon overrun by Sardinian, English and Russian troops under the command of Cardinal Ruffo, and the Bourbons, protected by Nelson's fleet, returned and reoccupied their capital on 13 June 1799. The return of the Bourbons was the signal for a terrible massacre of the liberal elements in Naples.

Two years later Napoleon came to terms with the King of the Two Sicilies, and undertook to withdraw his garrisons from south Italy if Ferdinand would stop the Allies using the ports of his Kingdom.

But in November 1805, Maria Carolina came to an understanding with the Allies, and 14,000 Russians under Lascy, plus 10,000 English under the command of Sir James Craig and Sir John Stuart, the future victor and Count of Maida, landed at Naples. At this, Napoleon angrily sent from Schoenbrunn the famous dispatch dispossessing the Bourbons, and stated "*que la Reine devait attribuer sa ruine à sa dernière perfidie*".

The French armies marched on Naples, where they were joined on 14 February 1806, by Napoleon's brother Joseph, and with General Portonneaux hammering at the gates of the city, a general evacuation began, the Russians leaving by land while the English embarked their troops on the fleet anchored off Castellammare. On 12 February, Ferdinand and Maria Carolina, carrying with them the state treasures and their furniture, had fled once more with the court to Palermo, and their troops retired to Calabria. On 15 February, Joseph entered Naples, and French troops occupied all the islands in the Bay except Ponza, opposite Gaeta, which was defended by the Prince of Hesse-Philippsthal, a courageous German general and son of the Landgrave William II, who had remained faithful to the Bourbons.

By a decree of 30 March, Joseph was elevated by his brother to the throne of Naples.

This marks the beginning of an epic struggle centering around Capri, a struggle which, before ending in a useless Napoleonic victory, enlivened the history of the island with many an amusing incident.

The new turn of events in the Kingdom of Naples was not to the liking of its English protectors, and caused many sleepless nights to Lord Collingwood, the Commander-in-Chief of the Mediterranean Fleet. At the beginning of May 1806, he dispatched a squadron under the command of Sir Sidney Smith to reprovision Gaeta, and to do what it could to upset the French occupation of Naples.

This brought on to the Capri scene some of the leading characters of the *grande époque*. Lord Cuthbert Collingwood had flown his flag on the *Royal Sovereign* at Trafalgar, where he commanded the second line of battle, and on Nelson's death had taken over command of the fleet. Sir Sidney too was an old acquaintance of Napoleon's, having been his chief stumbling-block in the Egyptian campaign; he has gone down in history for his defence of Acre, which caused the failure of the French plans for the conquest of the Near East. Speaking of him later at St Helena, Napoleon exclaimed: "*Cet homme me fit manquer ma fortune!*"

The gallant Sir Sidney, having completed his mission at Gaeta, led his forces in the direction of Naples with the idea of carrying out a nuisance raid on the city. But on entering the Bay of Naples on 10 May, he found the city illuminated and given over to festivities—celebrating with a solemn *Te Deum* in the Church of the Holy Spirit, amid the "delirious" enthusiasm of the people, the proclamation of Joseph Bonaparte as king. According to the *Annual Register for 1806*, the hero of St Jean d'Acre was touched at this sight: "It was in the power of the English admiral to have disturbed their festivity; but, as the sufferers from his interference must have been the inhabitants of Naples, and not the French troops, or the new king, he wisely and humanely forbore, and made for the isle of Capri; of which he took possession...".

From his flagship the *Pompée*, anchored at Scalea, in the Policastro roads, Sir Sidney Smith on 24 May 1806, wrote a detailed report for Admiral Lord Collingwood on the operation carried out at Capri. The event is also described in the official report of Captain L'Etang, who took over the command of the island after the glorious death of his superior, Captain Chervet.

In accordance with the usual practice of the times, Sir Sidney Smith began by politely but firmly calling on the French to surrender. To this Captain Chervet tersely rejoined that a true soldier only surrenders after he has tried his strength against the enemy.

There ensued a graceful bombardment with cannon-balls and grape-shot, to which the French politely replied *par une vive fusillade*. A landing was then effected by Captain Hannus, with a party of Royal Marines. Finding his way barred by Chervet in person, Captain Hannus, from point-blank range, fired a shot which stretched the gallant Frenchman dead at his feet. Captain L'Etang, discovering that he had been taken in the rear by troops landed from the *Athénienne* at the Piccola Marina, handed over his sword, and the flag of His Britannic Majesty was hoisted on Castiglione, renamed Castle Hill.

News of the grave rebuff suffered by French arms at Capri was communicated by King Joseph to his Imperial brother, and in return Joseph received a cutting little lesson in insular strategy: "I could have told you what would happen to you at Capri. When dealing with an isolated island, there is only one principle to follow: either put a lot of troops there, or none at all".

It would have been better for the English if they too had heeded this lesson.

After this successful attack, Sir Sidney Smith returned to Sicily, leaving behind on Capri a provisional garrison of 200 men. In consultation with the commander of the English troops in the Mediterranean, Sir John Stuart, it was decided to turn the little island which had been so easily conquered into a formidable fortress, making it at the same time the principal centre of information in the theatre of operations which were destined to halt the triumphal march of the unconquered Corsican. And since the idea was to defeat Napeoleon wherever he showed himself, Capri was to be the stronghold from which to fight him at Naples.

Looking round for a man capable of maintaining his position on the very doorstep of Napoleon's new kingdom, the political and military chiefs with one accord nominated Lieut.-Col. Sir Hudson Lowe.

To be wise after the event is easy, and this coupled with the unfavourable judgment of the great military critic and historian Sir William Francis Napier, and the unenviable task entrusted to Lowe by the English government of being Napoleon's gaoler, have all contributed to diminish the military stature and obscure the personality of this excellent officer who was first, Governor of Capri and later, of St Helena. Lowe was born in 1769, the year which also saw the birth of Napoleon, Wellington, Castelreagh, Lannes, Soult and Ney. An ensign at 18 in the 50th Regiment of the Line, he served with distinction in Italy, Egypt and Germany, and was always to be found fighting honourably wherever his country was in conflict with the French. He had also done garrison duty at Aiaccio, on Elba and at Lisbon. Perhaps it was at Minorca that he first had the idea of an Intelligence Service, for Minorca was the refuge of Corsicans and other political exiles whom England tried to use against the French. Lowe also showed himself a good organiser and an excellent disciplinarian, in fact, the perfect martinet. For his military virtues, he was given the job of forming the Corsican Rangers; for all his many other qualities he received the commission of turning Capri into an impregnable stronghold and a centre of espionage.

In his task of making Capri a "Little Gibraltar", Lowe chose as his collaborator a daring and unorthodox officer, Captain Richard Church, who was later to become one of the outstanding military figures of his country.

Church was of Quaker stock, but finding the religious practices imposed on him by his family uncongenial to his spirit, he ran away from home and took the King's shilling, enrolling as a volunteer. Later he was reconciled with his father and, buying a commission, he began in 1800 his adventurous and successful military career and covered himself with glory at the battle of Maida.

On his arrival in Capri he threw himself with ardour into the construction of the island's "impregnable" fortifications, which were much praised by the senior Engineering Officer of the British forces in the Mediterranean and singled out by him as models of their kind. In his letters to his family, Church gave a vivid account of his activities. Though scornful of the enemy's deeds of daring, he continued for his own part to embark on dangerous and sensational escapades. According to his own account, he had a passion for Ariosto, and some of the spirit of the *Orlando Furioso* seems to have entered his correspondence. He rhetorically describes the great volcanoes of the Mediterranean, Etna, Stromboli and Vesuvius, as erupting in amazement at his prowess, while the story of his deeds is studded with reminiscences of classical mythology, of which to some extent Church saw himself as a continuator.

From his description, the topography of Capri seems to consist entirely of precipices, cliffs and abysses; only if a mountain is practically perpendicular will he deign to climb it; one day, noticing that the only means of communication between the two ends of the island were the steps cut into the sheer rock by the Greeks, he climbed them one by one on his charger, "a light, spirited Arabian horse".

Meanwhile King Joseph, angered by his defeat and still more by Napoleon's ceaseless promptings to do something about Capri, sent an expedition under General Merlin to attempt the reconquest of the island. But Hudson Lowe had been warned of this attack by his spies, and had no difficulty in driving off the French. He then continued to build up his defences with men and arms, and to bring his system to perfection. But his espionage activities were destined to give him considerable trouble.

Napoleon, feeling that he could not entirely rely on his brother at Naples, had sent to him as minister in charge of police the famous Saliceti, a Corsican friend of Napoleon's youth, who had protected him at the outset of his career and who had been one of the great names of the Revolution. Hudson Lowe on his side also employed a Corsican, Antonio Suzzarelli. Suzzarelli, a rogue and scoundrel, had made himself out to be a lawyer and a former English officer, and had succeeded in winning Hudson Lowe's approval. He became Lowe's right-hand man, and was entrusted with the organisation of espionage at Naples. One day the French stopped a ship bound for Capri, and when the cargo was confiscated, Saliceti found that in addition to supplies—for the larder of Sir Hudson—it contained a compromising message from Suzzarelli. Surprised to find a Corsican in the enemy's service, Saliceti suggested to Suzzarelli that he should work for him as well as for the British, and from that day forth the French police at Naples were unseen participants in all that went on at Intelligence Headquarters on Capri.

But Suzzarelli was playing, and playing perfectly, a double game—deceiving, with cool effrontery, both the

English and the French. In this he was assisted by the famous President Vecchioni, one of the Counsellors of State of King Joseph, who invented the stories which were to deceive both Palermo and Naples.

At Naples, manifestos appeared on the buildings calling on the population to revolt against their French oppressors, and false information was supplied to the *Monitore*, which was consequently known to the Neapolitans as *'u giurnale d'e papocchie*—the newspaper of trash. A flotilla under the command of a certain Bruno and containing a group of "pirates", among whom was the famous Gallo, known as the "Deaf Man of Praiano", slipped through the French blockade round the island, and carried out continual raids on Naples. On one occasion a gang of desperadoes landed under cover of darkness, assassinated a senior police official and returned unmolested to Capri.

One of the people who passed through Capri was a Bourbon officer called Gumminelli, who with the aid of a certain Mosca was planning to assassinate King Joseph. Hudson Lowe was shown the credentials given him by Queen Maria Carolina, together with a bracelet entwined with a lock of her hair and a written promise to make him a colonel if he were successful. But Gumminelli was betrayed in Naples by his mistress and hanged.

In his *Memoirs*, written a few years later at St Helena, Hudson Lowe noted that all the would—be assassins of Joseph and his ministers had passed through Capri.

But the Queen had other uses for the devoted Governor of Capri; through him she kept herself supplied with all the latest French fashions on sale in Naples, even going so far as to ask on one occasion for some expensive watches. The agent for all these transactions was the ubiquitous Suzzarelli, who, according to Lowe, took a commission of a hundred per cent for his services. No wonder Sir Hudson complains bitterly in his *Memoirs* about the enormous sums he had to spend on his secret service!

But perhaps he did not know, or did not like to mention, that there were other "services" which Suzzarelli had rendered him. For Suzzarelli was running with the hare and hunting with the hounds, and it was only right that he should sometimes do something for Saliceti. Finding at Naples a teacher of English who had a certain talent for forgery, he got him to write a letter in Hudson Lowe's handwriting containing scandalous remarks about Maria Carolina. The letter, a masterpiece of malice and spite, was smuggled through to Palermo and shown to the Queen. The English high command was immediately bombarded with demands for the dismissal of the Governor of Capri, and the latter, faced with the evidence of the false handwriting, was hard put to it to prove his innocence and placate the wrath of the Queen. This was only one of many tricks played on Lowe by Saliceti and Suzzarelli.

Apropos of the gullibility of the Governor of Capri, Barry E. O'Meara, Napoleon's surgeon on St Helena, tells the following story in *Napoleon in Exile*: Saliceti used to amuse himself by listening to Antonio Suzzarelli's stories of the subterfuges and tricks he had played on Lowe, and one day he said to him, "I'm beginning to find it hard to believe in this famous colonel of yours; nobody could be so stupid! I would very much like to meet him!" "Colonel Lowe", replied Suzzarelli with dignity, "is not stupid; it is I who am clever!".

An attempt was actually made to arrange a meeting between Saliceti and Lowe at Naples. Hudson Lowe was to go there in secret, to see the lie of the land, and was to put up at the house of a spy called Maresca; and while he was there Saliceti was to visit the house, making out that he was a spy in the service of Suzzarelli. But at the last minute Sir Hudson, not trusting

Maresca, gave up the idea. He would have been quite safe; Saliceti had undertaken not to arrest him, for it would be impossible, he said, to get another Governor who was so easy to deceive.

But Hudson Lowe was not quite as stupid as Saliceti would have liked. In the second year of his Governorship he foresaw changes in the Kingdom of Naples, and correctly guessed that the French would try to reconquer the island of Capri. He therefore reinforced his garrison, hurriedly completed his fortifications, and as senior officer in Anacapri replaced the clever and fiery Church with the gallant Major John Hamill, another heroic veteran of Maida. In September 1808 the garrison of Capri consisted of 20 companies, or 1800 men, from the Royal Malta Regiment, the Royal Corsicans and the Watterville Regiment, plus 150 Marines and an adequate supply of artillery—with the result that according to Colonel Brice, Chief Engineer Officer of the British forces in Sicily, the island was impregnable.

Among the Lowe Papers in the British Museum there is a document which shows that, in the event of an attack on the island, the Governor had thought of everything. A week before the attack was launched Suzzarelli was charged with restocking the Governor's cellar with some French wines, which had arrived in Naples for the king's table: four dozen bottles of Champagne, three dozen of old Burgundy, and three dozen of the best wines, such as Frontignan.

In short, everything on Capri was ready for the French.

Having removed King Joseph from Naples by forcing him to accept the throne of Spain, which all his other brothers had refused, the Emperor wrote on 2 May 1808 to his brother-in-law, Joachim Murat, Lieutenant-General of his Armies in Madrid, "promoting" him King of Naples. By a decree of 20 July, he was declared to have ascended the throne of the Two Sicilies, as King Joachim Napoleon. He entered Naples in triumph on 6 September, and in his first message to the Emperor announced: "*Je ne désespère pas de pouvoir bientôt annoncer à Votre Majesté la reprise de Capri*".

On 18 September Napoleon replied, "*La prise de Capri serait d'un bon résultat: elle signalerait d'autant mieux votre arrivée qu'elle ferait craindre aux Anglais pour la Sicile, qui serait utile*".

The dashing and heroic assault and landing of the Franco-Neapolitan forces of King Joachim Murat at Anacapri on 8 October 1808, and the subsequent surrender of the English on the 16th, ratified on the 18th, have their usual complement of official and historical literature, but have not yet received the treatment they deserve.

The English version of these events is contained in the *Journal of Occurrences durin the Enemy's Attack on the Island of Capri*, an unpublished account now in the British Museum. In the French war archives there are detailed reports from Murat presenting the French side of the picture; and for Italians there is the account in the *Storia del Reame di Napoli*, by Colletta.

Historians and military critics may perhaps be interested in Sir William Napier's opinion of Sir Hudson Lowe, described as a man who "became known, for the first time in history, by losing in a few days a position which he should have held for many weeks". Others will prefer something less depressing, for example the epic poem *La Presa di Capri* by an obscure priest of Anacapri, Don Antonio Farace, which had the honour of being translated into English by Sir Lees Knowles, Baronet, C.V.O., O.B.E., T.D., D.L., M.A., LL.M., and was published in a magnificent *de luxe* edition with Italian and English text.

This little poem reveals that in placing all his trust in the formidable artillery with which Hudson Lowe had provided his strongpoints on the island, Colonel

Brice had been somewhat too optimistic. The good Don Antonio, faithfully translated by Sir Lees, recounts an episode in which this artillery, going into action to repel an attack on Renticale, did not function as it should have done:

> ...a little gun
> On land began to fire; another piece
> Was aimed o'er Renticale, but such force
> It used in firing that it broke in two
> And, with the charge yet in its paltry trunk
> Fell rolling down, and sank into the sea:
> Who could refrain from laughter at this sight,
> Though sign it was of sorry times to come!

Another who witnessed the French reconquest of the island was Tito Manzi, a lawyer attached to police headquarters in Naples, and a protégé of Saliceti. Tito it was who, when asked, along with other experts, for his advice on the expedition's plan of attack, suggested they should land in the direction of Limbo, where the coastline terminates in a series of almost unscaleable rocks, and for that very reason would be less likely to be defended. This choice was accepted by Murat, and explains why the evening before the embarkation of the expeditionary force all the lamplighters of Naples were ordered to bring their long ladders to the Arsenal, where they were loaded on to the flotilla of military transports which was about to set sail for Capri.

It also explains why historical pictures of the epoch represent the commander of the expedition, the famous General Lamarque, in full-dress uniform, leading his gallant men up a lamplighter's ladder and on to the rocks of Anacapri, to be met by a hail of smallarms fire directed by the equally gallant Major Hamill.

Fortunately these episodes of martial valour are interspersed with others not recorded in the *Fastes de la Gloire*. For example, we read in the annotations to a fragmentary copy of Farace's poem, now in the Biblioteca Caprense, that when the French reached the gun emplacement on Mt Cetrella and turned the cannon they found there on to the Palazzo Inglese, where the Governor was living, his cook was running round the kitchen garden trying to catch a turkey for the evening meal. With the first shot they fired at Capri—a fireball—the French hit the turkey and deprived the commander of the enemy troops of his supper.

Realising the gravity of the situation, Lowe decided to abandon the Governor's palace; and, retiring within the walls of Capri, he installed himself in the Palazzo delle Case Grandi, now Cerio, near the church, and there, with his customary sangfroid, he sat down to await the arrival of the fleet, which had left Sicily at the news of the French landing in the hope of relieving the island.

Several days later Hudson Lowe was standing at a window talking to his faithful servant Nicola Morgano, who was behind him, when suddenly he received a blow from Morgano which sent him sprawling to the ground. "God damn you, Morgano. Have you turned traitor?" cried the Governor, raising himself on one arm. At that moment one of the window panes was shattered by a bullet, and Morgano was saved the trouble of explaining that he had seen the crack marksman of a French reconnaissance patrol take aim at Sir Hudson.

With this blow Morgano, in a humble way, enters history; for, it can be argued, if there had been no blow and the bullet had found its mark, the fate of Napoleon on St Helena would have been less grim. For it was Sir Hudson, as Governor of the island, who was responsible for the conditions in which Napoleon lived, and he certainly saw to it that they were none too pleasant. He took every opportunity of humiliating the Emperor and making life difficult for him, and consistently refused to acknowledge his former "Majesty". Thus, whenever he presented himself to the Emperor in order to announce some new restriction, he always concluded by saying, "*Entendu, Monsieur le Général Bonaparte?*". To which Napoleon invariably replied, "*Entendu, Monsieur le Héros de Capri!*".

One final, literary, digression. In 1905 Joseph Conrad, ill and worn out, apparently by the effort of writing *Nostromo*, came to Capri, and remained there for four months. An account of his stay can be found in the letters published in G. Jean Aubrey's *Joseph Conrad, Life and Letters* (Heinemann, 1927). Imagining what a masterpiece the famous story-teller could make of the materials in my Biblioteca Caprense concerning the Anglo-French occupation of Capri, I offered them to him for his use.

Conrad gave the matter serious consideration, and wrote about it to his agent Pinker, pointing out that a book on Naples, Capri and Sorrento, places much frequented by English and American tourists, would stand a better chance of popularity than his other works.

But while all this was going on he began to arouse the interest of Edmund Gosse, the librarian of the House of Lords, poet and critic, and of the Prime Minister, Arthur James Balfour, the scholar and statesman who was to become one of the most enthusiastic Conradians of the time. Through the intervention of these two eminent men, Conrad obtained a pension on the Civil List, and, having successfully resolved his financial difficulties, he abandoned the idea of a book with a Capri setting, and, returning to England, began to write the novel which at that moment was uppermost in his mind, *The Mirror of the Sea*.

The Taking of Capri, 1808: (*Above*) General Lamarque, the first to land on the island. (*Below*) The French troops using the ladders of the lamplighters of Naples. Both pictures reproduced from *Les Fastes de la Gloire*

Drawing by C.W. Allers (1891)

CHAPTER VII

KLEIN DEUTSCHLAND

With the execution on 13 October 1815 at Pizzo di Calabria, of Joachim Murat, Marshal of France and King of Naples, there ended the period known to Italian history as the *decennio francese*, the ten years of French rule in the Kingdom of Naples.

About ten years later Capri became the scene of a farce entitled "The Discovery of the Blue Grotto". This was preceded by "The Disappearance of the Grotta Oscura". On 15 May 1808, the entrance to this Grotto, the island's greatest scenic marvel, had been blocked by a landslide on the hill of Sama, near the watch-tower of the Certosa. The praises of the Grotto, commonly accepted as the scene of Tiberius' wildest orgies, had been first sung by Capaccio, and then by famous English and French travellers. Its loss had to be supplied, and this task was undertaken by the notary Don Giuseppe Pagano, a lawyer and wielder of the pen no less inventive than his father Don Michele, the author of the posthumous will of Thorold.

The charming house of the Paganos, situated on a property of theirs where even today *die Zitronen blühn*, had been for some time past a most inviting and acceptable hotel, and at the turn of the century housed the neo-classical poets Stolberg, Stegmann, Rückert and Platen, and the painters Hildebrandt and Blechen, all visiting Italy in the footsteps of Goethe.

Only in August 1826, however, with the arrival of two painters, August Kopisch and Ernst Fries, did it seem to Pagano that the time was ripe for him to put into practice his little scheme.

Kopisch had not only the physique, but the mentality of the typical foreigner who shows perpetual astonishment at the wonders of the island. The islanders themselves, though accustomed for centuries to the astonishment of their visitors, are congenital cynics whom nothing ever surprises; but they expect the foreigners who land on the island to be surprised at everything. So it was with Kopisch and Fries when, putting up at the small but already famous hotel, they began to receive lessons from the notary Pagano in Roman antiquities, Tiberian atrocities and Capri superstitions *ad usum barbarorum*.

Their astonishment was first provoked by the learned hotelier's little library, well stocked with the classical authors, who from the earliest times showed a marked tendency to interest themselves in Capri: Homer, who made it the dwelling of the Sirens; Virgil, who recounted the story of Telon and the nymph of the Sebeto, and Statius, Pliny, Silius Italicus, Juvenal, Dio Cassius, Strabo, Seneca, Tacitus, Suetonius. These last two had much to say about the immorality and cruelty of Tiberius, but Don Giuseppe Pagano was even better informed.

It was generally held on the island that the most elegant debauches of Tiberius had taken place in a large and awesome cave by the sea. While staying incognito at the Palazzo delle Dame Occulte (the modern Damecuta is held to derive from this name), Tiberius gained access to this grotto by a secret passage (locally thought to be the *cloaca maxima* of Anacapri). And there he disported himself with nymphs procured for him by that instrument of the devil Nevius Sertorius Macro, at Rome Prefect of the Praetorian Guard, but at Capri promoted to the highest office in the Court, Provost of the Imperial Pleasures.

All this, and more besides, Don Giuseppe Pagano told his guests, and anyone who wants to know what else he said should read *Die Entdeckung der Blauen Grotte* (The Discovery of the Blue Grotto), by August Kopisch, which appeared twelve years after his Capri adventure.

In addition to what might be called its classical elements, the tale of the notary Pagano also contained some even more dramatic material drawn from local tradition. The poor, timid islanders, those *wunderglaübige Italiener* whom Goethe had seen perched on the rock of Tiberius, had never had the courage to penetrate into the fearful Grotto, because its waters were inhabited by an evil spirit said to have assumed monstrous human form, in their belief, Glaucus, son of the sea-god, Poseidon. A short while before, however, Pagano said an audacious fisherman, famous for his skill as a harpooner of tunny, had dared to go right up to the entrance to the mysterious cave in pursuit of an enormous fish which was trying to escape. At the touch of his harpoon, this creature's body had emitted a flood of blue light, thousands of intensely blue scales had floated away in the water, and the monster had slowly vanished. So at long last Glaucus had been killed, freed from life amidst a shower of blue, and those who had the necessary courage could now explore his cave, and find the traces of the misdeeds of Tiberius.

But only two sentimental Germans, more daring even than the fisherman, only Kopisch and Fries could undertake the task of rediscovering the Blue Grotto. Accordingly, on 18 August 1826, these two, accompanied by their host Don Giuseppe Pagano, and guided by the harpooner of Glaucus, Angelo Ferraro, known as il Riccio, *discovered* the Grotto of Gradola, well known to all the fishermen of Capri, and christened it the Blue

Grotto. The baptismal certificate is to be found in the Visitors' Book of the old Albergo Pagano, still preserved by a descendant of Don Giuseppe in another hotel of the same name.

The most extraordinary thing about the discovery was that nobody took any notice of it. It was not until two years later that a friend of Hölderlin, the young poet Wilhelm Waiblinger, who had been sent to Italy by the famous publisher Cotta, turned up on Capri, and after initiation into the mysteries by the notary Pagano, composed a poem with the Blue Grotto as a setting. When he had finished this wonderful legend, *Das Märchen von der Blauen Grotte*, he insisted on its being read to the people of Capri; the reading took place after a Gargantuan feast staged by Pagano among the ruins of Villa Jovis, at which the fame of the almost unknown German poet was greatly enhanced by the enthusiasm of the guests, who naturally had not understood a word.

But the legend, one of the minor and least attractive works of Waiblinger, was a success in Germany, where in the meanwhile the praises of Capri had been sung by Count von Platen in the idyll *Die Fischer von Capri*, which appeared in 1827, and is still numbered among the glories of German nineteenth-century lyric poetry. In 1835 the seal of fame was set on the discovery of the Blue Grotto by an indifferent novel of Hans Christian Andersen, called *Improvisatoren*. Only when the Grotto had already become famous, through the literature which had accumulated concerning it, did Kopisch remember that he had discovered it, and in 1838 he published in Berlin his *Entdeckung*, a Capri classic which nobody nowadays ever thinks of reading. At the beginning of this century, when it was suggested that the centenary of the exploit of Kopisch and Fries should be celebrated, an article appeared called "How the Blue Grotto was not discovered", in which an attempt was made to dispose of the myth most dear to the hearts of the *pallonisti*. In the local language *pallone*, literally a balloon, is a yarn spun for the delectation of the credulous foreigner. As for the *pallonisti*, they are a corporation of fishermen who specialise in catching—visitors; their victims, taken on a conducted tour of the island, have ample opportunity to admire two of its most outstanding charms: the truly wonderful spectacle of its many natural grottoes, and the astonishing inventive powers of the inhabitants.

The fact that the Blue Grotto was not discovered in 1826 is amply proved bya map of Capri in the magnificent *Isolario*, published in 1696 by Coronelli, Cosmographer to the Venetian Republic. The now famous grotto is the biggest of the many marine caves, and the one in which, as is shown by the ruins which have been found there, the Romans must have had one of their so-called nympheums—places which were set aside for various pleasures, mainly gastronomical.

When the *Sturm und Drang* movement, that fermentation of the spirit inspired in Schiller, Goethe and Herder by the idealism of Rousseau, had come to an end, the young demigod Wolfgang received a revelation from his learned and revered father, Counsellor Goethe: he who has seen Naples and its surroundings can never be entirely unhappy. From this article of faith was born the *Italienische Reise*; and the romantic route to the world of the classics which this work mapped out was soon thronged by hordes of painters and poets, hungry for beauty and unable to resist the call of the South. The advance guard took Capri by storm, and after the discovery of the Blue Grotto proceeded to conquer the rest of the island with their art, their poetry and their good humour.

The first groups of German intellectuals established at Rome at the beginning of the nineteenth century were the painters who called themselves "Deutsch-

Römer", led by Cornelius, and the "Nazarenes", headed by Overbeck. Both these schools had ramifications at Capri, where Von Führich came to draw his illustrations for the *Märchen* of Waiblinger. But the island had its own group of artists and poets, calling themselves "Die Odysseer" to mark their admiration for the world of Homer. The members of this group are entitled to be called the founders of the first German colony—if only a purely spiritual one—*klein Deutschland*, which lasted for almost a century, from the "discovery" of the Blue Grotto until the eve of the First World War. More than three-quarters of Furcheim's *Bibliographie der Insel Capri* (1916) is taken up by Germans; recently Claretta Cerio, a student of German at the University of Naples, wrote a thesis on "A century of German poetry on Capri", which contained a bibliography of 144 writers; and this does not take into account the geologists, zoologists, botanists and various other German authors, to whom the greater part of the scientific literature on Capri is due.

But the Germans who visit Capri today have never heard of many of these writers. People still read the Idylls and the Eclogues of Count von Platen, but the *Fragmente über Italien* by Stegmann is a bibliographical rarity, and as for the poetic *Briefe aus Capri* and the *Lied an Capri* which Waiblinger composed on his deathbed at Rome at the age of 26, it would not be surprising to find that Capri is the only place where these works are still known.

Another prominent German visitor was the composer Felix Mendelssohn Bartholdy, who in 1830 stayed at the Albergo Pagano, which at that time was, as it were, an outpost of the "Nazarenes". Mendelssohn left a poetic description of the Blue Grotto which can be found among his *Reisebriefe*, and during his stay on Capri also composed the *Walpurgisnacht*.

The German conquest of the island, which started

at the beginning of the nineteenth century with the Goethian "Odysseer", was completed towards the middle of the century by a new invasion of historians and writers, among whom it is only necessary to record those who have left a lasting impression on the history of German literature.

In 1851 the historian of medieval Rome, Ferdinand Gregorovius, wrote a tragedy set in Capri, *Der Tod des Tiberius*. This was soon followed by *Capri eine Einsiedelei*, which, with the title *Idylle vom Millelmeer*, was later incorporated into the *Wanderjahre in Italien*, one of the masterpieces of descriptive literature.

In March 1853 there landed on Capri an unknown lawyer called Victor von Scheffel, who shortly after his arrival composed a poem featuring Capri, *Der Trompeter von Säckingen*, which in the space of six months made him the most popular writer in Germany and the idol of the students. At the beginning of this century the golden jubilee of this book, written in the Albergo Pagano, was celebrated by the printing of its three hundredth edition; to find a copy today you would have to go to an antiquarian bookseller. If you were to ask a young German whether he had heard of the book which had been a best-seller when his grandfather was young, he would probably answer: "Scheffel... Scheffel... never heard of him! Who was he?"—a question doubtless echoed by many of my readers.

He was a plump, fairish gentleman with a comfortable middle-class air. One of the heroes of his poem was a cat, Kater Hiddigeigei, who philosophised on the roof of the Albergo Pagano. This cat gave his name to a famous café, the "Zum Kater", which became, and remained until 1914, not only an emporium of English groceries and German *Delikatessen*, but a permanent exhibition of local paintings, a rendezvous for all the chatterboxes of Europe, and all the geniuses, understood and misunderstood, who came to Capri for solace and inspiration.

Around its tables gathered a distinguished throng of writers and artists, politicians and men of science, discussing, wrangling, brooding over their misfortunes, or more simply drowning their sorrows in beer and whisky: Booth Tarkington and Joseph Conrad, Hindenburg and Masaryk, Lenin and Gorky, Von Lüdendorff and Krupp, Gerhart Hauptmann and Ellen Key, Rainer Maria Rilke, F. Scott Fitzgerald, Sinclair Lewis, Sudermann, Bismarck's doctor, Schweninger, Chaliapin, Bashilov and, in a corner reserved for his guests, Sir Compton Mackenzie, at that time the brilliant author only of *Carnival* and *Sinister Street*, discoursing, in the manner of the true aristocrat of letters, on anything but literature.

All this, and much more, took place in the restaurant which Victor von Scheffel had suggested to its owner should be called after his learned cat, Hiddigeigei.

The "Little Germany" which flourished on Capri at the end of the nineteenth century was a perfect replica of a Fatherland that was now well on its way to a hitherto unknown prosperity.

In addition to its material prosperity, the second Reich was in the full flood of a renaissance comparable to that which a century before had given to Europe the genius of Goethe. A new impetus was given to letters and the arts, which were encouraged, but at the same time tainted, by the vainglory of the Kaiser. The German people, fortunately for them, were vouchsafed the blessing of a great humorist, Wilhelm Busch, who prevented them from taking themselves too seriously. Unfortunately he did not have the same effect on Wilhelm II.

Contingents of scientists, geologists, botanists, doctors and biologists arrived on Capri for rest and meditation as can be seen from the pages of the bibliography

104

of Furcheim. Masters and disciples filled the tables of the Kater Hiddigeigei. Emil von Behring, the "Children's Saviour", as Pasteur called him, came to Capri after quarrelling with his chief, Robert Koch, and bought a villa—later Lenin's "Red House"—where he used to spend one half of his double life. At Capri, under the influence of Schopenhauer and Hartmann, Behring devoted himself to metaphysics, writing treatises on the *Problem of Death* and the *Problem of Life*. After frequenting the island for about twenty years, he noted in his diary, at Villa Behring, on 1 August 1912: "*Metaphysik ist Bedürfnisfrage*"—"Metaphysics is a question of need". But he never had time to develop this concept, for he became entirely absorbed in those vital studies on tetanus, which had already brought him a Nobel Prize, and, in the First World War, were to give him a new title—the "Soldiers' Saviour".

Among other visitors were a joyous company of artists, poets and novelists presided over by Hans Barth, the author of that masterpiece of *Kneipenpoesie*, or "poetry of the tavern", known as *Osteria*, a cultural and historical guide to all the wine-booths of Italy, from Verona to Capri. Its itinerary was subsequently completed by Norman Douglas' *Alone*, which contains perhaps less poetry than Barth's work, but more gay erudition.

By the end of the nineteenth century the German colony on Capri, encouraged by the local inhabitants, who derived much financial advantage from it, had become all-powerful. At its stronghold, the old Albergo Pagano, the Kaiser's birthday, 27 January, was celebrated as one of Capri's national feasts, with the participation of the local authorities. The main road of the island was called Via Hohenzollern, and the most picturesque spots on the island all had their German names: *Malerplatte*, *Die Terrasse* (Tragara), and so on.

A new band of artists was formed calling itself

"Homeric", to distinguish it from the somewhat too conventional Nazarenes. Members of this group included a well-known and successful sculptor of the period, Hoffmeister, the architect Weichardt, who had planned, and hoped to carry out, the reconstruction of the main Augusto-Tiberian villas, the portrait painter Streitfeld, the landscape painter Rettich, the historical painter Lang, and a specialist in battle scenes Von Willewald. The group also included the Englishman Adrian Stokes. Their emblem was the staff of Bacchus, which they carried in procession round the island before going to perform their pagan rites at Pizzolungo, where the group, spiritual descendants of the "Odysseer", venerated their patron Polyphemus.

But these performances, which bore a marked resemblance to the ceremonies in honour of San Costanzo, aroused the suspicions of the Church, and the feast of the Homeric Cyclops had to be celebrated in the hall of the Albergo Pagano.

With the support of the authorities and of leading figures on the island, a society was formed with the imposing name of *Capriverschönerungsverein*, the Society for the Embellishment of Capri. The moving spirit was a certain Schreiber, a hellenist who hoped to restore the island to its Greco-Roman glory, with colonnades of fake marble, artificial temples and similar amenities in the style of Alma Tadema. An attempt was made to get the Kaiser to build a little "Achilleion" on the plateau of Monte San Michele, an estate which the Commune were to offer to the Hohenzollerns so that Capri might once more become Imperial.

When the island was at the height of its Teutonic splendour, there burst upon the scene the painter C.W. Allers, who had appeared a few years before like a blazing comet in the firmament of late nineteenth-century German art. Allers, a remarkable master of line, had had the good fortune to catch the eye of Bismarck, and

106

had been invited to stay at his retreat at Friedrich-sruhe, where he had drawn the Iron Chancellor in every conceivable pose and humour.

He brought with him to Capri a great stock of portraits, not to mention various little belongings of Bismarck, such as pipes, sticks, beer mugs, discarded berets and other odds and ends, enough to send into raptures the devotees of the Founder of the Empire.

Building himself an ugly villa on Via Tragara, Allers made it a model of the style of time; and with the superabundance of furniture which that style demanded, and the piles of relics he had brought away from Friedrichsruhe, it soon became a sacred temple where Germans, far from their homeland, could worship their idol without fear of offending the Imperial iconoclast.

Villa Allers, externally tending towards the local style, was internally the very epitome of German cosiness, that perfect synthesis of every material discomfort to which Germans of that period were so attached: imitation Renaissance furniture, twisted and contorted; medieval arms and armour; heavy tapestries and hangings. In the centre of the main wall hung Allers' masterpiece, a large head of Bismarck.

The height of *Gemütlichkeit*, however, was reached in the garden. Here, for the ladies of the German colony, addicted to coffee-parties, was the *Gartenlaube*, the arbour, while for the men, naturally more inclined to philosophical speculation, there was a discreet *Trinkecke*, or drinking corner. But the garden's crowning glory was the bowling alley, the *Kegelbahn*, the Mecca of all the Germans in the Mediterranean.

Between 1890 and 1900 all the eminent Germans whom we met at the Albergo Pagano and at Kater Hiddigeigei visited Villa Allers: Sudermann, Fulda, Hans Heinz Ewers, Meyerheim, Schoenleber, Hindenburg...

During the ten years of his stay, Allers painted the

portraits of many of the notables of the island. At the same time, he went around Capri, Naples and the surrounding area drawing, with his extraordinary facility and an almost mechanical speed and perfection, practically everything he came across, views, people and things, above all scenes of real life, which he had himself observed in the streets and cafés and other frequented places.

Many of these drawings are reproduced in two large and very rare folio volumes, *Capri*, published at Munich in 1892, and *La Bella Napoli*, published in 1893, at Stuttgart.

At the same time, he also filled the walls of *trattorie*, barbers' shops and cafés in Naples, Sorrento, Ischia and Capri with innumerable drawings of Bismarck; which were all stupidly destroyed, in an access of mistaken patriotism and out of hatred for the Germans, during the First World War.

Accused of immorality by an intending blackmailer, Allers left Capri in 1902. Hoping to live down the scandal by disappearing, he buried himself in Samoa, and was quickly forgotten. When he returned to Germany from New Zealand he was unknown, and in 1915 he died, aged 58, at Karlsruhe, where thirty years previously he had been a student at the Academy of Fine Arts.

One of the chief characteristics of this German renaissance was the importance now allotted to science rather than to poetry. Side by side with the dynasty which had given to the Germans their third Emperor, there had come to power another dynasty, that of Fire and Steel. At the beginning of this century a new monarch was proclaimed: the King of Guns, Friedrich Alfred Krupp, a gentle and kindly man singled out by a cruel and ironic destiny to put into effect, with the industrial and financial power of his firm, the dreams of grandeur of his friend, debtor and lord, Wilhelm II.

Krupp came to Capri inspired by the oceanic researches of Professor Chun, and full of enthusiasm for the work of Anton Dohrn, director of the Zoological Station at Naples, the first marine biology experimental unit, and a meeting-place of the leading investigators of the mysteries of underwater life.

Up till then, the study of the minute organisms which had eluded the first deep-sea researches had been held up for lack of funds. Krupp, stepping into the breach, fitted out two boats for this special type of deep-sea fishing, the *Maia* in 1901, and the luxurious British yacht *Puritan* the following year, and in two memorable expeditions made a notable contribution to deep-sea biology, discovering a large number of new species, and revealing among other things, the possibility of animal life below 1,800 feet.

Thus, in the waters around Capri, Krupp and the *Puritan* brought to completion the great cycle of deep-sea researches undertaken by Great Britain with the *Porcupine*, the *Shearwater* and the *Challenger*; by America with the *Albatross* and the *Blake*; by Germany with the *Valdivia*; by Italy with the *Washington*; and by the Prince of Monaco with the *Hirondelle*.

But in the Bocche di Capri, Krupp had a fortunate encounter; down in the depths, he came across a creature resembling a desiccated willow-leaf: *Leptocephalus brevirostris*. Salvatore Lo Bianco, the brilliant classifier of the Zoological Station, a great friend of Krupp and the man who was always urging him to undertake further underwater research, discovered that *Leptocephalus* was none other than the larva of the common eel. With this discovery it became possible to reconstruct and establish the life cycle of the eel, a fish which is part of the traditional Italian Christmas fare, and one of the most important products of shallow—water fishing in the Mediterranean basin, and also to solve the mystery of its migratory habits, which take it from the rivers and shores of Europe to the Sargasso Sea.

Air de Capri, air de souci, so indeed it proved at the beginning of the century, for the Germans, for the Kaiser did not approve of their squandering their fortunes in a land of perdition.

The numbers of foreigners increased. Maxim Gorky arrived with his rich and generous publisher and patron, Piatnitzky, and around these two there began to form a court of high-ranking revolutionaries.

Of the Germans only a few princes remained—the Grand-duke of Hesse, a Schaunburg-Lippe, one of the many Reuss. Perhaps it was the assurance of being received by a small *élite* that induced Rilke to leave his ivory tower in the North and come to Capri. In Paris, at the time of his association with Rodin, he had been considered the leading poet in Europe; he had founded and permeated with his aristocratic spirit the artistic group of Worpswede. Among the aristocracy of France, Germany and Austria he had his own private chorus of admirers, none lower in rank than a countess!

Rainer Maria Rilke came to Capri in the stormy winter of 1906-7, and spent many months there without anyone noticing him; indeed, we could aptly apply to his stay on Capri a remark made about him by his great friend, Stefan Zweig, in *World of Yesterday*: "Peace formed itself around him wherever he went or happened to be". In this peace he worked hard, writing several poems and many letters, which can be found in his published correspondence. But he remained completely unmoved by, and absolutely impervious to, the natural beauties of the island. The enthusiasm of foreigners for these beauties exasperated him; from his own opinion of Capri one would imagine that all he knew of the island was the area centering on the Piazza and bounded by the main *alberghi*. "This place has become what it is", he wrote, "through some extremely misguided enthusiasm".

Not once during his stay did Rilke try to get the feel of the landscape, or put himself in touch with the soul of the people. In his letters he complains about everyone and everything. He reproaches the island for having too many hills in too small an area: "*zu viel Berge auf zu engem Raum*". He even complains about the sea; a serious defect, this, for an island, to have so much sea around it: "sea wherever you go, sometimes on one side, sometimes on another, sometimes on both sides at once".

In a letter to Leonida Pasternak, he also complains about Gorky: "Gorky has settled here amidst the acclaims of the socialists and splashes his money about all over the place". In another letter he says, "People here, having become accustomed to Diefenbach's ostentation, are now having to get used to Gorky, who lets himself be fêted as an anarchist and then cheerfully doles out money to all and sundry". As Gorky was a generous man who entertained at his own expense dozens of Russian refugees, mostly intellectuals, it was particularly objectionable of Rilke to couple him with Diefenbach, a German painter who prostituted an undoubted talent by his aggressive exhibitionism, and who tried to turn Capri into a temple of the pan-germanic cult, thereby giving the island a foretaste of the Hitlerian folly.

How can we explain the bad temper of Rainer Maria Rilke at Capri? Although the much-admired Ellen Key was a fellow-guest in the house in which he stayed, he did not find himself surrounded by the usual number of countesses; in fact, his hostess was only a baroness. He had the good fortune to be able to dedicate his poem, the *Migliera*, to Countess Manon von Solms-Laubach; but the *Feigenbaum*, a poem inspired by the splendid fig-tree which grew in such a romantic manner beside the little church of Sant'Andrea, at the

111

Piccola Marina, brought only misfortune, for the majestic tree, overcome by the honour of being celebrated by one of the great names of modern German poetry, withered up and died.

If only out of vanity, the author of these chronicles also likes to number among the most precious jewels of German poetry the poem dedicated to him by Theodor Däubler, who was for many years a resident on Capri.

Of his amazing epic of the Nordic race, *Nordlicht*, Däubler himself said to a friend shortly before his death, "The work which I have completed surpasses all other works by human hands; I have imparted a concept of Being, which finally, after all the doctrines of annihilation, leads the soul upwards; I have taught that the mechanical law which produces life lies in the fact that the earth itself brings forth the forces opposed to gravity and tends towards a return to the Sun".

But the man who thundered with the voice of Jupiter and preached a "return to the Sun" spoke to a people who could not answer him.

At the beginning of this century Däubler was one of the leading poets of Germany; academic honours showered upon him, and he was numbered in Athens among those who laboured for the resuscitation of the ancient spirit of Greece.

Much of the last period of his life was spent on Capri. Finally he left for the Black Forest, where he died in a sanatorium in 1936. His importance as a poet is still to be decided.

Caricature of Tristan Corbière by himself

Alfred Krupp

Chapter VIII

PARNASSIANS ABROAD

In the early nineteenth century the forerunners of the "open-air" school of painting began to frequent the island; they later became the so-called School of Posillipo: Giacinto Gigante, Consalvo Carelli, the Neapolitans Fergola and Cammarano, and the famous landscape painters, Duclère and Pitloo, who were living in Naples. Their works are best seen in the collection in the Museum of San Martino.

Recently there has come to light in London a picture containing a view of Monte Solaro, painted in 1828 by Corot, who lived on Capri at the same time as Gigante. There is no written evidence of the visit of this great French landscape painter, and of other famous artists of the period, but a glance through the art galleries of France shows works such as the *Combat de Coqs* by Gérome and *Les exilés de Tibère* by Barrias, which have Capri as a background.

The island made its entry into nineteenth-century French literature in the works of the great novelist Alexandre Dumas *père*, who first appeared on Capri in 1835, with the artist Louis Godefroy Jadin. Of this first visit Dumas gave a detailed account in a book which is today almost unobtainable, *Le Spéronare*, published in 1841. The title is derived from the word *speronara*, which means a type of sailing boat usually used for transporting cargo, but also suitable for carrying passengers. Havin hired one of these boats in Naples, the celebrated novelist and his unusual cook Monsù Cama, who had a passion for reciting the *Orlando Furioso*, landed at the Grande Marina, and came upon a man stretched out asleep in the sun, "a new Christopher Columbus who lived on an income which arrived in his sleep". It was none other than Angelo Ferraro, called il Riccio, the man who had harpooned Glaucus, the companion of August Kopisch on his famous voyage of discovery, the fisherman who was now unemployed. Riccio, in fact, proclaimed by the islanders the real and only discoverer of the Blue Grotto, had succeeded in obtaining a small pension from the Government, and he enjoyed it sleeping on the beach, dreaming of the famous discovery he had so daringly made, and which he was always ready to relate. He told the story, of course, to Dumas, who described the Grotto as "*une immense caverne toute d'azur come si Dieu s'était amusé à faire une tente avec quelques restes du firmament*". Dumas' imaginative description is full of random excerpts from the classics badly remembered, and pieces of information supplied by il Riccio. In addition the novelist took the opportunity of introducing into his account a discreet number of historical and archaeological blunders, and thus, having made an involuntary contribution to the humorous literature about Capri, he departed on his ship for his fantastic Mediterranean cruise.

When he reappeared on Capri after 1860, the author of *The Three Musketeers*, on the strength of the help he had given Garibaldi during the liberation of Sicily, had been appointed to the post of Director of Antiquities in Naples. Here Dumas had founded and was running a newspaper, *L'Indipendente*, at the same time that his collaborators were compiling the novels set in Naples with which Dumas enriched his already vast production. At Capri lived his most industrious and learned collaborator, the famous archaeologist

Cavaliere Carlo Bonucci who, faithful to the cause of the Bourbons, had resigned from the management of the Excavations of Pompeii, and had then retired to Capri, where he lived in poverty.

During the first half of the century Bonucci, famous for his learning, had acted as guide to sovereigns and all the celebrities of the age, and had inspired many of the works of art dealing with Pompeii, for he had a talent for evoking its ancient way of life. In Bonucci's papers, some of which are still preserved on Capri, there are notes of his meeting with Edward Bullwer-Lytton, for whom he provided the historical material for *The Last Days of Pompeii*, and with Byron, in whose presence he directed the excavations of the House of the Tragic Poet; and recollections of Lamartine, Delavigne, of the Countess of Blessington, of Thiers, Cambronne, Canova, la Malibran.

Amongst these papers is also preserved an autograph letter from Alexandre Dumas dated January 1861, which fixes the terms of a payment for the text of the work published by the *Indipendente* as *The Bourbons of Naples by Alexandre Dumas*.

In 1869 one of the most outstanding painters of the Roscoff group, Tristan Corbière, made his first appearance in Capri. Tristan had started as a painter and caricaturist, but later revealed his real talent as a poet with *Les Amours jaunes*. Of the artistic activity of Corbière in Capri, after the destruction of the decorative panels which he painted in the Albergo Pagano, there remain only the caricatures he drew in the hotel registers.

Among the painters who came to Capri was J.J. Henner, who won the Prix de Rome in 1858, and who is remembered for his landscapes of the island. Others who followed him were Edouard Sain, colleague in Rome of Carolus Duran, and called in Paris *le peintre des Capriotes*, Jean Benner and his son, Many, who had been born in Capri, Bonneau and the whole group of artists who in the second half of the nineteenth century saw themselves, if only jokingly, as the spiritual founders of the *École de Capri*, whose productions for almost half a century never failed to enliven the annual displays of painting at the Salon.

If almost all these artists came to Capri to set out on the road to fame, and many of them gained notoriety there, one of them, called *'U Francesiello*, came to the island in order to be forgotten. And in fact for many years no-one knew who Camille du Commun du Locle was or what he had done in France, and it was only at his death that his life became known. He was born in Orange in 1832, completed his education at the *École des Chartes*, and came to Italy on winning the Prix de Rome for palaeography. Attracted to the theatre, he began his dramatic career with a comedy, *M'sieu Landry*, and later established himself as a writer of librettos for Duprato. With Méry he wrote the libretto of *Don Carlos*, and afterwards that of *La Forza del Destino* for Verdi. In 1871 he became director of the Opéra Comique, and played an important part in the musical and theatrical life of France, collaborating with Meyerbeer, Halévy and Auber. After the musico-religious expedition of the Saint-Simoniens to the East, he visited Egypt, and was commissioned by Mariette Bey to write the libretto for an opera glorifying the land of the Pharaohs, which was to be performed at the opening of the Suez Canal. From this was born *Aïda*, at first intended by the Egyptian Government to be set to music by Wagner, but which Du Locle succeeded in obtaining for his friend Giuseppe Verdi. The triumph of the opera, performed on 24 December 1871, in Cairo, was also shared by the librettist, who had given Verdi the opportunity to branch out in a new direction, to free himself from the influence of Donizetti and to introduce a new technique which employed the massed orchestra and revealed the melodic richness characteristic of his genius.

As for himself, Camille du Commun du Locle had his own triumphs, with a prize from the Academy of France for his *André Chénier*. Suddenly, however, at the height of his fame he disappeared from the Parisian scene and came to Capri, as he said when dying, "*pour finir mes jours en fare d'une eternelle* première".

In the spacious non-Catholic cemetery, known in the literature of Capri as the "dynamic cemetery" because of the frequent movement of bodies from one tomb to the other, a short distance from the tomb of Du Locle rises the tombstone of Fersen.

On Capri, they like to believe, if only out of courtesy, that in November 1923 a poet died, just as in Paris they liked to believe that a new poet had been born when in 1901 there appeared the *Chansons légères* by the young Jacques Adelswaerd Fersen. One of the creators of this impression was Edmond Rostand, who wrote in the preface to the volume of verse: "*Je vous félicite d'être un Adelswaerd et d'être un poète. Il est bien, que les dernières gouttes d'un sang chevaleresque fleurissent poétiquement*". Rostand was referring to the blood of the noble friend and defender of Marie Antoinette.

But Jacques preferred to claim spiritual parentage by calling his second book of poems *Hymnaire d'Adonis à la façon de M. le Marquis de Sade*, in which he revealed his true colours as a decadent and a retarded parnassian with *Adonis aux yeux clairs* and *Paganismes*.

Having made his début in the manner of the Marquis de Sade, Baron de Fersen attempted to emulate the English "decadents", notably Oscar Wilde, and tried to revive in Paris the medieval Black Mass.

But a fate similar to that of Wilde befell Fersen. He was tried and condemned, and after a few months in prison, undertook a long journey to India, China and

Japan. When he returned to Europe he came to Capri, where he received a more favourable welcome than that which met Oscar Wilde, who came to Capri in 1897. When Wilde entered the dining-room of a large hotel, all the English people present, in fact almost all the guests, rose to their feet, scandalised, and threatened to leave the hotel if it gave shelter to him, and Wilde retired to Paris, bitterly complaining of the welcome he had had in Capri, where even bread had been refused him.

Fersen appeared unexpectedly, flashing with riches, and installed himself for a while in the Certosella, the beautiful villa built by Du Locle. Since he had had the good taste to restock its cellar with the most valued wines from the French vineyards, and to install there a chef said to have been a pupil of Escoffier, his début in Capri society was an enormous success. Soon, however, he felt the need for a home of his own, far from the tourist traffic and from the curiosity of local society. So he built himself a house on Mount Tiberius, a little below Villa Jovis, calling it first La Gloriette and then Villa Lysis; and there he retired, as he confided to his small circle of chosen friends, in order to write poetry in perfect solitude for the rest of his life. At the Villa Lysis, Fersen assembled his valuable collections of Chinese curios, and a precious collection of jade, and installed an opium den which immediately won him new renown. But when the object of this renown was identified with the priest of the famous Black Mass in Paris, a certain perturbation could be noticed in the ranks of polite society on Capri. The force of this disapproval eventually compelled him to leave the island.

Fersen returned, however, after the First World War and devoted himself to the writing of poetry. His one passion in life was now typographical precision.

The poet would send his works to be printed, but having received the first proofs he would virtually tear them to pieces. He would wait for the second proofs, and then set furiously about correcting them. Then he would send them back to the printer, and await the third lot with trepidation... and then the fourth, and then the fifth... He was still young, and he was spurred on by the hope that one day he would be able to give the poems his approval, his *imprimatur*.

That day finally came, but when the work was printed, new troubles arose; fresh misprints invariably sprang forth. And so he struggled to the very end; with every new work a typographical torment, which racked his very soul. And finally, death, a sad and miserable death.

But not even in the non-Catholic cemetery could the refined aesthete find peace. On the small grave-stone which covers his tomb are engraved the words

JAQUES ADELSWAERD DE FERSEN

Final, supreme sadness; fearful nightmare: *Jacques* without the *c*!

Jacques Fersen and Nino Cesarini

Chapter IX

OLD ENGLAND

When I was still very young—I might have been seven or eight hours old—I played a part in the history of the island which might have had serious consequences.

I came into the world at dawn on a very warm summer's day. By eight o'clock the excitement caused by my arrival had died down, the bedroom in which the happy event had taken place had returned to normal, and I, tightly enveloped in swaddling clothes, like one of the mummified cats which sleep the everlasting sleep in the tombs of the Pharaohs, slept my first sleep beside my mother. Of the events which followed I have no personal recollection: *relata refero*.

My father, a volunteer who had served with Garibaldi, had remained in the Reserve of the Italian Army with the rank of captain. On Capri, he had two jobs: doctor to the Commune and medical officer to the Fifth Provost Company billeted at the Certosa, and every morning at nine he would put on his uniform to go and take the sick parade, returning at eleven to change into civilian clothes for the morning surgery.

And so, on the morning of my birth, reassured by the profound sleep into which my mother and I had fallen, my father donned his uniform, buckled on his sword, and went off to the Certosa, leaving the bedroom in shadow and the faithful Mariuccia on guard at the door.

A little before eleven we were aroused from our slumbers by the despairing cries of Mariuccia: a man was trying to push his way into the room, quietly but firmly insisting, in English, on being allowed to congratulate my mother and baptise me.

Mariuccia defended the door as long as she could, but in the end she had to give in, and the man entered our room brandishing a bottle of champagne and shouting: "Hurrah!".

It was Mr Burton, the black sheep of the English colony on Capri. With a great effort my mother raised her head from the pillow, pointed with her outstretched arm to the door, and said firmly and distinctly: "Sir!".

But Burton was undismayed: he ordered the terrified Mariuccia to bring two glasses, removed the wire round the top of the champagne cork, and started to explain his idea.

There were, according to him, too many Christians in the world, too many spoilsports, The only hope of salvation lay in a return to paganism, and, being himself already converted, he was on the lookout for proselytes, for, like so many other Englishmen who have come to Capri animated by the Messianic spirit, he not only preached but practised his religion.

Being on friendly terms with our family he had decided to do us a good turn as soon as he heard the news of my birth; baptise the new baby with the Bacchic rite. It was all very simple: just sprinkle a bit of champagne and give the child a symbolic name.

Having explained all this at great speed to my mother, he asked her to choose for herself the name I was to have. Dionysus? Perhaps that was expecting too much. Better the name of a satyr—Silenus. Burton would take care of my education, would bring me up— Silenus, from the time he was small, had been the inseparable companion of Bacchus.

With a loud report the cork shot out of the bottle,

and Burton began to sprinkle me with the foaming liquid. I started to bawl, my mother disappeared beneath the bedclothes, and Mariuccia made a genuine effort to faint. At this precise moment my father entered the room. His first impulse was to run the Englishman through with his sword. But with his hand already on the hilt, he hesitated, remembering that he was an officer: the honour of a soldier demanded a more official satisfaction. The insult which he had received would indeed have to be avenged in blood, but the blood would have to be shed in a regular manner, in a duel.

When the Captain of the Certosa and a lawyer expert in affairs of honour, acting as my father's seconds, delivered to Burton the official challenge, he rephed, diplomatically, with the *fin de non recevoir*, refusing to nominate his seconds. His conduct was naturally considered insulting to the bearers of the challenge; and, in accordance with the code of honour, they were obliged to resign their office and in their turn send their seconds to Burton, who was apparently ignorant of even the most elementary rules of chivalry.

The incident provoked by my birth was beginning to assume alarming proportions. Even the Mayor, charged with the maintenance of law and order, began to be concerned. On Burton's side there was the British Vice-Consul at Naples, behind whom it was easy to see the influence of the Foreign Office, at that time all-powerful in the Mediterranean. Fortunately, a friend to both sides, the well-known painter, Talmage White, took it upon himself to adjudicate the controversy, and the matter was amicably settled over a round of drinks at the Anglo-Saxon Grocery Store, then the main café in the Piazza. As a result, Mr Burton and my father became even greater friends than before.

The Anglo-Saxon and its café were the advance post of the British colony on Capri, in rivalry to the

Kater Hiddigeigei, the rallying-point of the German element in the Mediterranean. Its owner, Don Antonio Scoppa, who also ran the mail-boat service, combined the functions of general *factotum* for all the foreigners on Capri with those of banker to the "remittance men". The banks of Rome and Naples transmitted to him, and he passed on or administered to their recipients, the cash allowances paid to men of quality by their families in Britain to keep them out of the country. This system kept the level of morality among good society in Britain high and constant, but had an unsettling effect on British society at Capri, which was divided into those who were respectable but dull, and those who were entertaining but dissolute.

The "good society" had its headquarters at the splendid Villa Castello, home of Mr and Mrs Walter Anderson, *At Home Thursdays*, as their visiting card explained, and indefatigable organisers of garden-parties and many other social activities. The Andersons were artists. Sophie Anderson was a tall woman of imposing appearance, who was generally known to the natives as the Cauliflower Lady, because of her magnificent head of white hair, which reminded them of the illustrations of cauliflowers, of the variety *Magnum bonum*, which they had seen in the horticulturist catalogues. But in addition to her hair-style, Mrs Anderson was also famous for her painting. Her pictures were shown in London, at the Royal Academy, and it was possible to come across reproductions of them anywhere in the United Kingdom. Herself an enthusiastic reformer, she had undertaken first and foremost to reform the nude in art.

Mrs Anderson knew how to confer on the nude all the finest human qualities, while eliminating those attributes of the flesh which are the damnation of man. In fact, it was flesh which was at the centre of her reform of painting. For its representation she had a very simple chromatic formula of her own: silver white, just a touch of chrome yellow and pink lacquer mixed with carmine. Treated thereafter, as only Mrs Anderson knew how, with successive glazings, the flesh she depicted could be enjoyed in perfect safety, as one enjoys a de-nicotinised cigarette, or a cup of coffee minus the active elements of caffeine. It was un-aphrodisiacal; it had no carnal savour, no appetising quality. It could never be confused with the flesh painted by Titian or Rubens. Sophie Anderson, in a word, succeeded in making classical art presentable even in the most proper of Victorian drawing-rooms.

Using the famous Capri models, whose comeliness and generous proportions were a byword among other artists, Mrs Anderson yet managed to produce subjects of an unusual grace and dignity: Andromeda, Iphigenia, the Three Fates, the Cumaean Sibyl, Circe...

I recall with some emotion one of her masterpieces, Cupid and Psyche.

A little before the last war, I was visiting the cathedral cities of England, and arriving late one evening at Wells, decided to spend the night there. Finding a picturesque little inn in a lane behind the cathedral, I went in, and was astonished to see the walls of the hall covered with a collection of fine prints. The hostess, a spotlessly clean and very polite old spinster, at first eyed me with suspicion, and on hearing me speak, inquired anxiously: "A foreigner?". I managed to reassure her and she, seeing my interest in her pictures, offered to show me them. I recognised at once Iphigenia, and was delighted to hear my hostess explain: "By Sophie Anderson, my favourite painter!".

Happily I looked around, hoping to revive other memories. There was Millais' *Ophelia*, drowning in a sea of brocade, more than anything else, for the waters of the stagnant, weed-choked pool would probably only have come up to her knees. Then came a whole series of Landseers; and after them, an old acquaintance, *The Monarch of the Glen*. Suddenly I started, seeing a picture I had completely forgotten: the beautiful shady courtyard of Villa Castello, and in the background a large jar with an oleander in flower. Seated on the edge of the jar, Eros, with his quiver on his back and two glittering little wings attached to his shoulders, was feeling with one small finger the point of an arrow and looking meaningly in the direction of Psyche, concealed behind a splendid specimen of *Philodendron speciosa*, which, however, scarcely sufficed to hide the charms of the rival of Venus.

"My favourite picture!" explained the landlady of the little inn. Pointing to the naked and winged infant, I asked her if she knew who it was. Blushing a little she replied, "Cupid, the God of Love!". "No!" I said, "that's me!".

The old lady gazed at me, incredulous—she saw a fully dressed man, with a grizzled beard, no wings, no quiver; then she shook her head and decided that she did not have any room for me in her inn.

I would have liked to explain that until I was five or six I too had posed for Sophie Anderson, and always in the same costume: bow, arrow and wings.

But what would have been the use?

Sophie Anderson's reforms covered not only art, but also life, particularly the social life of Capri. In this she had an enthusiastic collaborator in her husband, Walter Anderson. A painter, too, though not a great one—he measured little more than five feet three inches—he devoted himself to *genre* painting; his pictures were not exhibited at the Royal Academy, like his wife's, but were sold to an art dealer in Bruton Street. He painted subjects from the Greco-Roman world, though not so well as Alma Tadema. Sometimes his pictures were reproduced in *Sunday at Home*.

128

Because of his passion for correct behaviour he was naturally considered his wife's chief supporter in the campaign for the reform of manners conducted from Villa Castello. It was he who sent out the invitations for the garden-parties, he who called on new arrivals, only leaving his card, of course, with those of unimpeachable reputation. As a consequence the social functions of Villa Castello were attended by Protestant clergymen of various denominations, retired Civil Servants, Anglo-Indians and other colonials, well-connected spinsters of a certain age who drew butterflies and flowers, or botanised—and only a handful of artists, those whose artistic views were not too extreme.

At the big strawberries-and-cream party in the spring, when there was a preview of the works Mrs Anderson was submitting to Burlington House, and those her husband was sending to his Bruton Street dealer, all the guests wore a primrose to show their adherence to the ideals of the Primrose League.

This gathering was the occasion of a two-fold orgy, an orgy of nudes and scenes of Roman life in the artists' studio, and then an orgy of strawberries and cream in the garden.

One of the people who were never invited to these little celebrations was Mr Burton; but one year, that of the anniversary of the Cauliflower Lady's first show at the Royal Academy, he decided to invite himself. When he arrived the paintings had already been admired, and the garden-party had reached its most animated stage, with the guests tucking in with a will in the garden. Crossing the courtyard, Burton went up to the front door, rang the bell and waited. Everybody was in the garden, so he had to wait some time. At last the maid arrived. She opened the door, took one look at Burton, and fell senseless to the ground. Burton had nothing on! And thus he appeared, a few moments later, on the garden terrace, before the startled gaze of

English society on Capri. Burton may have been a rake, but he was also a fine figure of a man; and the young ladies present, after having a good look—so that they might be properly scandalised—bolted the strawberries and cream which remained on their plates, and fell in a swoon on their chairs. Mr Anderson, with some willing helpers, threw Burton out, barred the door, and then had a stroke of genius—possibly the only one in his life, and certainly the most inspired. Going to his little workshop he took a large drill and drilled four holes in the top panel of the door of Villa Castello.

From that day on, whenever there was a ring at the front door of Villa Castello, the maid who ran to answer looked first through one hole, then through another, then, to make assurance doubly sure, she looked through the other two holes as well, and only when she had made sure that the caller was not completely naked did she open the door.

These holes soon became famous, and are remembered as the Holes of Mr Burton.

Various circumstances have conspired to create the legend, handed down to us by a tradition still alive among the inhabitants, that true love on the island is only found at Anacapri. One of the contributory factors was certainly the raids of the Barbary pirates, the principal object of which was to carry off the most beautiful girls of the upper territory to fill the harems of the African coast. Words cannot describe the success of the girls of Anacapri after Gregorovius, in his charming *Idylle von Mittelmeer*, had described them as perfect examples of the Greek ideal of feminine beauty. Impersonated by Rosina, a famous model, their beauty charmed Queen Victoria, who insisted on buying the portrait that Sargent painted of this girl. Anacapri subsequently became the source of the most beautiful models of the *École de Capri*.

Thus it is not surprising that Burton, when he realised that he did not yet have an *innamorata*, made Anacapri the first port of call on his journey to the kingdom of Love. He took his time, had a good look round, thoroughly explored the neighbourhood, and one evening, on his return to the Caffé della Piazza, was able to give his friends the news of his discovery, Luisa, the daughter of Mastro Saverio, the baker.

Mastro Saverio, the baker of Anacapri, was a happy man. Although he had been left a widower when he was young, with four small girls to bring up, he had had the good fortune to see them grow up around him in such beauty as to be christened the Four Seasons, for at Anacapri the seasons of the year are each more beautiful than the other, like his daughters. Then, too, the girls helped him in all his work. This was not confined to the art of baking, for like any self-respecting mastercraftsman, he also owned a bit of land, enough to keep his family as their position required: a small vineyard and an olive-grove, a rocky pasture for the goat, some arable land and a garden; and naturally the little threshing floor for threshing the buck-wheat, an oil press, a wine-cellar, and of course the bakery itself, built with his own hands and provided with every contrivance the ingenuity of man could devise, not only for making bread of every kind, but also for producing any piece of fancy baking which might occur to the master-baker's fertile and inventive mind.

But with four daughters to marry off there was a serious problem to be resolved—that of the four trousseaux, all to be prepared from the hemp and flax grown on his own land, and woven, cut, sown and embroidered at home. So you can see that with the work of the bakery and of the land, the housekeeping and the loving labour of getting their trousseaux ready, the Four Seasons had little time for amusement, and it was quite an event if they were able to put in an appearance in some procession, walking behind the statue of the Madonna with the Children of Mary.

When Mr Burton appeared on the scene, the bakery of the Four Seasons was a great centre of attraction for the young men of the area, and Mastro Saverio, who was a great artist, was not averse to displaying his art to the young bloods of Anacapri, who would sometimes wait up all night in order to watch the removal of the bread from the oven, a ceremony on which the inspired baker conferred even greater charm by the preparation of *casatielli*, little loaves of maize mixed with oil and flavoured with raisins, which, when served by his beautiful daughters, made a delicious and unforgettable repast. Nor had these innocent orgies given rise to the least scandal, for the girls had always been able to keep their beaux in their place.

Of the four daughters of Mastro Saverio the eldest, Rubina, was engaged to a coral fisher, the third, Orsola, was being courted by a cousin, and even the youngest, Graziella, had a young man. Only Luisa, the second and the most beautiful of the Four Seasons, and her father's favourite, was without a swain.

After meeting her in the fields and exchanging a few words with her, Burton had tried other means of approach, but in vain. On hearing of his difficulties his friends suggested that he should try to forward his suit by calling in the help of art. The beautiful maidens of Anacapri were always willing to pose as models, for, sure of their charms, they knew that the painters would always end by marrying them. So Burton turned painter, and sent Luisa a love letter. But he was curtly informed that the daughters of Mastro Saverio only left their house to get married. By now the Englishman's whim had become a burning passion, and the next time he met Luisa he asked her to marry him. As if it were as simple as that! No! a matter of this importance could only be dealt with by her father, who had to be approached in the proper way, through the proper channels, by means of a suitable intermediary. Burton enlisted the services of the parish priest of Anacapri, who tackled Luisa's father. But Don Saverio showed himself absolutely obdurate. Yield the hand of his favourite daughter to a foreigner, particularly to a *fuggistenti*, a young man who had never done a stroke of work in his life! Never!

It was pointed out to him that the claimant to Luisa's hand was himself the owner of some lands, in the vicinity of London. But who worked them? Mastro Saverio knew only too well that lands not with one's own hands deteriorate, the vines go to rack and ruin, and the olive-trees run wild.

But then, when the young man appeared before him in person to plead his cause, so great was the passion he put into it, such was the grace with which he exalted the virtue and the charms of Luisa, that the baker's heart was touched, and he gave his consent to the marriage of his daughter to this *mauvais sujet* who had found some sense at last, and shown himself to be just a fine young lad, like anyone else.

So took place the marriage of Mr Burton to Luisa di Mastro Saverio, perhaps the most beautiful and certanly the best of the Four Seasons.

Renting a large old house with fields, garden and orchard, Burton put it into repair, redecorated it, and fitted it out with furniture sent from England. The daughter of Mastro Saverio, who was installed in this house like a queen, was given the title due to any woman who married a foreigner, and became Donna Luisa Burton; and the foreign colony, having seen so many good things come out of England, made a few careful inquiries, found that the lucky husband received an allowance from England to the tune of thirty pounds a month, and ended up by giving him the title he deserved: George Burton, Esq. Burton, full of good intentions, spared nothing to make life easy and pleasant for his wife, he engaged her a cook, chose her a maid. But Donna Luisa would have none of these amenities; somehow she could never bring herself to trust the servants, and she was always busy in the kitchen herself; it was she who crushed the tomatoes for the *purée*, she who salted the anchovies, and she who split the figs and put them to dry in the sun, nor would she let the cook have anything to do with certain stews which she prepared with her own hands for her husband.

Burton had had no idea that his wife had so many relations. Mastro Saverio belonged to the clan of "Fantasia", which occupied a whole quarter of Anacapri, and it was impossible to keep count of the relatives who, each in his own way, wanted to do honour to the Englishman. Fortunately, Burton soon showed that he was a generous man who knew how to repay people for their kindness. According to the season, a constant stream of quails, wild doves and woodcock flowed in to Casa Burton. Rosa the Cheesemaker, Donna Luisa's aunt, practised nepotism on a vast scale, and her numerous offspring were always arriving with presents of cheeses of various sorts, which were repaid with sugar, coffee and biscuits. One of Donna Luisa's uncles took possession of the vineyard, and another, Antolino lo 'Nzertatore, undertook to plant out the orchard with oranges and mandarins. In the midst of all these happy people the Englishman, who had married Luisa's clan along with Luisa, became happy too, and found out how to live. No longer was it necessary to indulge in scandalous behaviour to keep himself amused. The other reprobates of the foreign colony of Capri seemed to have quietened down too; the painters who had married their models were leading exemplary lives, and had even begun to be invited to Villa Castello. Reformation and counter-reformation had become fused; society on

Capri had changed out of all recognition: everyone seemed to be so well-behaved.

The Cauliflower Lady, now at the height of her power, decided to bury the hatchet, and asked Donna Luisa to pose with her three other sisters for an allegorical composition which would celebrate for all time the beauty of the four daughters of Mastro Saverio: *The Four Seasons*, Mrs Anderson's masterpiece.

Life in Casa Burton went on quietly and happily, and after a while the gossips who haunted the house all day were able to announce that God had blessed the union with the foreigner, and its fruit was now beginning to be manifest. But one day, out of the blue, there came a letter from England which threw the household into confusion and brought the charming idyll to an end. Burton had never spoken to his wife about his family, except to say that he was separated from them (he hoped) for ever. But fate had decided that this was not to be, that the idyll of Capri was not to last.

For George Burton was of noble birth, and belonged to a family which bore the title of Bentley, a little town with a castle, in Yorkshire. A cousin of his, the heir to the title, had died suddenly in a hunting accident, and George was now the heir. Donna Luisa was not very clear what all this meant, and at first was not particularly interested. All she wanted was to be left in peace. But at last it dawned on her that the death of this cousin would change her whole life: George would have to return to England, and she would have to go with him, becoming first Lady George Burton, and later, when her husband became a Peer of the Realm, Lady Bentley.

"*È un castigo di Dio!*" exclaimed the daughter of Mastro Saverio, and with Christian resignation she prepared herself for her fate. And thus, after an initial period of dismay, she accepted her new destiny: good-bye to the island, to her family, good-bye, Heaven alone knew for how long, to the village of Anacapri, the field of flax and hemp where her trousseau had grown; goodbye to the bakery, her married sisters, their little children.

Burton told her that she would also have to prepare herself for an audience with the Queen, and, resigned as ever, she submitted once more to the will of God.

The thing which most excited Capri about the future in store for the daughter of Mastro Saverio was this audience which Donna Luisa was to have with Queen Victoria. Burton, Lord Bentley, was not worried—by then Luisa's English would be a bit better, and in a big court function, all she would have to do would be to smile and, with her charm, everything would be all right. What could the Queen ask her, or say to her, except one of the stock questions or phrases, to which Luisa could reply with other stock phrases which she could easily learn?

But Capri, all Capri, almost, thought differently. The island was very concerned about making a good impression at the English court. All were agreed that in the little time which still remained to her on Capri Donna Luisa should try to improve her English, and it would be the task of the local doctor's wife, a thoroughbred Englishwoman, to instruct her in the language. But this was not all. The Parroco was very keen that she should know something about the history of Capri, and in this he found himself in agreement with a group of artists led by Talmage White. The latter proposed, and the other artists and the parish priest agreed, that Donna Luisa, or rather Lady Bentley, should be taught the history of Tiberius, so that she could tell the Queen of England what things had really been like, in the days of the Orgy of Capri. The example of Tiberius was one upon which every ruler should ponder.

Thus, from the Parroco's scraps of Roman history, and his rich stock of Capri lore, supplemented by information supplied by several of the less respectable painters, was compiled a picture of life under Tiberius *ad usum Reginae*. The initiation of the baker's beautiful daughter into court life had begun.

A frequent correspondence grew up between the bakery of the Four Seasons in Anacapri, and Bentley Castle in Yorkshire. The Parroco of Anacapri, who had taught the little Luisella not only her religion but also how to read and write, gave Milady regular news of the island and of her family, and regularly received in return the news from England, which he passed on to her father and sisters.

By now Lord and Lady George Burton had taken possession of their magnificent country house, with its estate of woods and fields, of whose richness nobody on Capri could have the least idea. In an immense meadow nearby scores of cows were grazing—a vision which brought to mind the arid hillside in Anacapri where Luisa had pastured her little goat.

There was as yet no talk of being presented at court, for the Queen, overcome by the terrible loss of the Prince Consort, had not returned to London.

The house was perhaps too big and silent, and Luisa was never able to explore it thoroughly, mainly because there was an uncertain number of servants and maids with whom she did not get on very well, for they refused to let her do anything. The kitchen was in the charge of a French chef against whom Luisa was powerless, and was practically out-of-bounds. The young mistress was watched over by a perfect butler, but he never succeeded in inducing in her that attitude of submission which all English butlers expect from their employers.

At long last the much desired son and heir arrived. Luisa would have liked to call him Saverio, but this was out of the question; he must be called George, for one day he too would be a Peer of the Realm, the thirty-second earl of Bentley.

The question of Luisa's presentation to the Queen was now reopened. But this was the beginning of further trials and tribulations. A new figure appeared on the scene, Lady Ann, Lord George's aunt, who assumed the role of preceptor to the infant, and incidentally to Luisa as well.

The presentation of Lady George, it was clear, would not take place in a crowded reception at the Court of St James, as was the usual custom, but in circumstances of the greatest intimacy, in Balmoral Castle, where the Queen had retired, to be alone with her grief.

However much her husband sought to free Lady George from the torture of Lady Ann, he was never successful. The unfortunate daughter of Mastro Saverio, the most beautiful and the best of the Four Seasons, was for ever in the clutches of this strict mistress of etiquette, who racked her brains to imagine the questions which the Queen might ask and to devise the answers which the young peeress from Anacapri could give; and as for the technique of curtsying, Luisa had practically to undergo a course of physical training in this subtle art.

At last came the invitation to Balmoral, that majestic pile of heavy Scots Baronial, which the Prince Consort had transformed into a love-nest, and where the Queen had passed the first years of her widowhood, in the most desolate solitude.

Before leaving Bentley Castle, Lady Ann organised a dress rehearsal of the presentation, which nearly drove Luisa out of her mind. Far into the night Luisa went on curtsying to the empty air, and trying to walk backwards after each curtsy in the direction of an open door—the hardest and most important part of an audience. This time the manoeuvre, which had always worked out well enough before, ended with her bumping into a doorpost. But at last the nightmare was over, and after a long and beautiful journey across England and Scotland in a coach-and-four the daughter of Mastro Saverio found herself on the threshold of Queen Victoria's private drawing-room.

It is not hard to imagine the scene: a room chock-a-block with uncomfortable armchairs, hard-backed divans and wobbly little tables, and full of mementoes of Albert, among which there was hardly any room to move; while near a large window, shaded by an array of curtains draped one on top of the other, sat the small, plump figure of the Queen, dressed in black.

Let us imagine, too, what happened on that occasion. At a nod from the Queen, Luisa advanced, terrified by the multiplicity of furniture, which stopped her from making any sort of curtsy in the manner she had been taught. Lady Ann, from behind, was directing operations with an energetic series of gestures; but her sign to Luisa to make her first curtsy almost brought disaster, for Luisa stumbled over a little table, and only succeeded in executing a graceful pirouette. When she drew near the Queen, the daughter of Mastro Saverio found the room she needed, and without waiting for the mistress of ceremonies, made a spontaneous and charming curtsy. Lady Ann, miming furiously, tried to remind her that she was supposed to take up a position beside the Queen. But charmed by the attractive *débutante*, the Queen took her by the hand and made her sit beside her, scarcely acknowledging the curtsy of Lady Ann, to whom she indicated a nearby seat.

Outside it was pouring with rain, and Victoria, alluding to the fact that there was a fire in the room, though it was midsummer, instead of addressing to Luisa one of the hypothetical questions imagined by Lady Ann, remarked, with the least regal and most natural air in the world: "What weather!".

At this Luisa, forgetting even Tiberius, and thinking of the drought which at that very moment would be tormenting Anacapri, replied "*Tutta grazia di Dio!* If only we had as much rain, where I come from".

This answer surprised and interested the Queen, because it referred to a living reality of which she was ignorant and which was far removed from the formal exchanges of these receptions. As a result, a genuine conversation began between the two.

"They tell me you come from Capri—a very beautiful island..."

"... if it weren't for this business of the water..."

"Are you short of water, then?"

"Very short, in the summer; and we have to go a long way to get it".

Getting more and more interested, the Queen asked: "I suppose you have a lot of water-bearers in your houses?".

Lady Ann made a whole series of grimaces, in an endeavour to suggest an answer to Luisa; but Luisa just burst out laughing: "Bearers, Ma'am? Wherever from? We go and get the water ourselves—I and my sisters, from an old Roman cistern at the bottom of the olive-grove of Tiberino...".

This reply threw Lady Ann into a fit, but it interested the Queen very much: "And does your family own some olives too?".

"Lots", replied Luisa proudly, with a certain amount of exaggeration, "one of the finest olive-groves in Anacapri!". Then, fearing she had overdone things in her praise of Mastro Saverio's property, she added: "With God's help, we have enough never to worry about being short of oil, and never to have to buy it. And we make all our oil ourselves...".

"Are you a large family, then?"

"Four sisters: Rubina—that's the eldest—married, with a lovely baby and another one on the way..."

Lady Ann, getting extremely agitated, tried to in-

140

tervene, but the Queen did not give her time, and with a smile asked Luisa: "And you?".

"One so far, a boy ... and you? A lot, haven't you?"

Without bothering about the unorthodoxy of the question, the Queen took several miniatures from a small table and showed them to her, explaining: "This is my eldest, Edward".

"Ah! you've been lucky too: a boy first!"

This remark provoked a gesture of despair from Lady Ann, but Luisa took no notice, all her attention being concentrated on admiring the miniatures the Queen was showing her. "What lovely children!" ("Princes", hissed Lady Ann) "How nice for you to have so many..."

Then the Queen picked up a larger miniature, showing the Prince Consort in the magnificent uniform of a Colonel of the Horse Guards, and handed it to Luisa. Admiringly, Luisa exclaimed, "Ah! your husband! What a handsome man!".

The Queen looked at her gratefully, her eyes full of tears, and Luisa, pressing her hand, added: "What you must have been through!".

By this time Lady Ann had practically passed out; but the Queen, who had lost the only man who could say to her: "Victoria, dear", had difficulty in restraining her tears, having met the only woman who had shown that she understood the Queen's great grief, and dared to say that she must have suffered.

And thus ends the story as it is told in Capri of the first conversation between Mastro Saverio's daughter and the Queen of England.

Chapter X

THE CRADLE OF THE RUSSIAN REVOLUTION

Before Maxim Gorky and before the colony of Russian revolutionaries and intellectuals which had formed itself around him at Capri in the early 1900s, another author, Ivan Sergeyevich Turgenev had come to Capri. Turgenev was the first of the great Russian novelists to be read and admired in Europe, revealing to the world the treasures of a new literature which until then had been ignored or misunderstood.

Turgenev established himself in Paris towards 1870, but in the following year, to escape the horrors of the Franco-Prussian war, fled to Germany. From Berlin he wrote to Gregory Danilevsky, a writer of historical novels, reproaching him for having passed a whole month at Naples without finding time to visit Capri. The island, he said, is a miracle, "a real temple of the Goddess Nature, the incarnation of beauty!". The letter ended with this prophecy: "You know, I am certain that before long the new generation of Russian intellectuals will choose the island of Capri as the goal of their pilgrimages, and, who knows, we might one day see there a strong Russian colony composed of painters and writers...".

Even before the eulogies of Turgenev, the beauties of Capri had been revealed to Russia by the great painter of seascapes, Aivasovsky, a pupil of Vorobiov. This successful and talented artist, who hailed from

Feodosia in the Crimea, rapidly made a name for himself and became prosperous through the sale of his youthful works. From 1840 to 1844 he was living in Italy. He worked with enthusiasm at Capri, where his art developed its characteristic realistic elements. The great gallery which he founded at Feodosia contains many of the seascapes he painted at Capri and at Sorrento, which he visited again towards 1870.

At Capri the glory of the Southern sun flooding over sea and hills presented Aivasovsky with a dazzling play of colours, and he found himself faced with problems of light of an intensity he had never before experienced. In search of a solution, he abandoned his studio and took to painting in the open air. A rapid and indefatigable worker, he amassed a great quantity of paintings drawn from nature, and on his return to Russia exhibited them at St Petersburg. But this time the judgment of the critics was unfavourable; the painter, they said, had been spoilt by his period of residence on Capri, and abandoning his usual naturalism, had employed imaginary colours of an impossible brilliance.

Grieved by this verdict he destroyed these studies from nature, and composed a series of views of Capri from memory, thereby establishing his reputation as a painter of seascapes.

With Aivasovsky at Capri was a great sculptor, Mark Antokolsky, who visited Rome in 1871, was well received and carried out important commissions there. On their return to Russia, both he and Aivasovsky became enthusiastic propagandists of the idea of Capri, encouraging artists and writers to visit the island. Between 1872 and 1880 many Russian intellectuals did do so, though without leaving any noteworthy traces of their visits.

Capri received a new and unexpected publicity through the publication of a novel by Vasili Nemirovich-Dancenco, a journalist who had travelled widely in

Italy, and who used the island as the setting of a sentimental novel which became very popular in Russia, and
inspired many artists and tourists to visit the places described by the author.

The propaganda begun by artists and continued by
men of letters gave rise at St Petersburg to the idea of
founding at Capri a *Ruski Dom*—that is, a house destined to receive Russian intellectuals in search of inspiration and rest—a sort of unacademic academy, to be
supported by public subscription, supplemented, it was
hoped, by a contribution from the State. Prince Tru-
betzkoi, the principal supporter of the project, laid it
before Alexander III, but the Tsar refused to collaborate.

From Rome, Venice and Florence, about 1900,
some of the most popular artists came to Capri: the
Sviedomsky brothers, Bacalovich, Bronnokov and Riz-
zoni among the painters; the historian Volinsky, and
the writers Mordovtzow, Boborykin and Merejkovsky.
Their sojourn on Capri left notable traces in the works
of all these artists, who contributed much to Russian
painting and literature at the beginning of the century.

After the conflagration which began with the
"Bloody Sunday" of 1905, those of the Russian intellectuals, who had been won over to the cause of Social
Democracy and compromised by the revolutionary ris-
ings, and who were able to leave the country took refuge in London, Paris, Lausanne, Geneva. But some of
the exiles, mindful perhaps of the enthusiastic descriptions of the writers, or dazzled by the luminous visions
of the painters who had come to Capri in the second
half of the nineteenth century, made that little island
their destination. Thus there came into being the
colony of intellectuals that Turgenev had dreamed of,
containing the flower of the *intelligentsia*—an *intelligentsia*, however, which was not bourgeois, as the old class

of culture and wealth had been, but socialist, in accordance with the intentions of Lenin.

One of the most influential revolutionary leaders involved in the insurrection of 1905 was Maxim Gorky, whose fame had already crossed the frontiers of his own country and made him the best-known living figure in Russian literature. Gorky carne to Capri and with him came Maria Fiodorovna Gelabuscskaia, the famous actress known as Andreeva, who became his companion and inspirer.

Maxim Gorky is chiefly known as a great and successful writer, but he also played an important and very lucrative part in the world of publishing. In the early years of the century Piatnitzky, a Russian of great learning and extraordinary business ability, and a devoted friend of Gorky, invited him to collaborate in the running of his publishing house *Znanie* (Knowledge), which specialised in the publication of literary works dealing with social problems.

Thanks to the efforts of the leading figures of the Italian Socialist Party, Gorky was received in Italy with honour and sympathy. At Capri he found a climate spiritually suited to his work and ideal for his health, for he was threatened by a lung complaint. Maria Fiodorovna was equally pleased: she found a society in which she could affirm both the sovereignty of her companion over the other *émigrés*, and her own sovereignty over him.

The incursion of Slavs, following on the heels of the great idealist and revolutionary, naturally came up against the usual migration of Germans, who since the beginning of the previous century had held complete sway over the island. The encounter, which resolved itself into lively meetings of all the foreign-speaking people on the island, took place daily at the café Zum Kater Hiddigeigei, whose importance to the German colony has already been mentioned.

Such was the society which greeted Gorky when he arrived with his first group of followers, among them Chaliapin. The great writer, the idealistic revolutionary, attracted into his orbit all those who were inflamed by the revolutionary spirit. The other Gorky, the former co-director of *Znanie*, and adviser on artistic matters to the famous publisher Piatnitsky, drew to Capri the Russian intellectuals—men of letters, philosophers, historians and artists. The first group of exiles which formed around Gorky and Maria Fiodorovna was a real intellectual *élite*. Its members included Leonida Andreiev, already famous in the world of letters, and the two Zolotarev brothers, one of whom, Alexis, a supposed anarchist with mystical tendencies, passed for a saint, while the other, a student of Italian culture, preached the gospel of Giordano Bruno, and translated his *Spaccio della bestia trionfante*. Others who added lustre to the group were the story-writers Izmailov and Gussev-Oremburgsky, Wolinsky, well-known for his studies on Leonardo da Vinci, and, later on, Lunasciarsky and the composer Tchaikovsky.

Maxim Gorky, while still a young man, had won fame with his short stories. When he came to Capri he had just severed his connection with the old *intelligentsia*; and initiated the proletarian period of his writings with his popular novel, *The Mother*, which was to make him the idol of the working classes.

This, the first book he wrote on Capri, turned towards him the anxious looks and the hopes of all the followers of the new religion. As a result a steady trickle of Russians arrived on the island, sometimes singly, sometimes in groups, eager to hear from the mouth of the new prophet the promise of better things to come.

The Italian government was at first worried about the influx of so many potential revolutionaries, and entrusted their supervision to an inimitable police officer, the Cavaliere Tiseo. Tiseo, however, was more interested in the safety of the Queen of Sweden, and gave all his attention to earning the order of chivalry which the Queen had promised him on condition that she was left in peace. As for the Russians, Tiseo said, they were an economic, not a political problem; and as much as could be done to help them had already been done by Maxim Gorky, who paid the debts of his fellow countrymen in the hotels and taverns, and put them up in his own house, when they had run out of credit.

Gorky's warm-hearted hospitality was made possible by the limitless generosity of Constantine Piatnitzky, who sacrificed all his energies to his idol, and put at his disposal the resources of his successful publishing business. Gorky himself was the first to recognise this; in his gratitude for his life of comfort, and for the opportunity it gave him of helping his friends, he wrote to Piatnitzky from Capri: " You are the mount on whose back I am allowed to ride so joyfully, and you do not even notice the burden you bear, so generous are you...". Gorky noticed the burden, though, and it distressed him, though he did nothing to curb the extravagant tastes of Maria Fiodorovna. Piatnitzky's generosity and her extravagance were the origin of another legend—the fable of the luxurious life and of the Gargantuan feasts of Gorky, and of the sumptuous and princely villa in which he was supposed to live.

The truth is that he first lived in a modest little villa on the hill which ran down into the ravine of Castiglione; then after a while he rented the larger and less attractive Villa Behring, the Red House, renowned as having been the site of the first (and perhaps imaginary) revolutionary tribunal, and later of the famous and more concrete revolutionary " school ".

The story of the first attempt at a people's tribunal arose from a tale put about by Gorky's faithful editor and patron Piatnitzky.

Fedor Ivanovich Chaliapin had arrived on Capri with the glory of his recent triumphs in Russia tarnished by the charge of having gone on his knees—he, a revolutionary—to render homage to the Tsar, while the orchestra played "God Save the Tsar" in the Imperial Theatre of St Petersburg, after a performance of Boris Godunov. For this he was to be tried by an improvised tribunal, meeting in the house of the great writer, for his "betrayal" of the cause of the revolution. It is hardly necessary to add that after a moving defence by Gorky on an enchanting moonlit night the trial ended with an acquittal. The rocks of the island were soon echoing to the Tartarian notes of the song celebrating the hatred of Boris, the greatest Tsar of Muscovy, for that brood of oppressors, the Romanovs.

Gorky was a life-long friend of Chaliapin, and the following tale of their youth was very popular in Capri: On one occasion when Gorky was travelling in the company of Chaliapin, the two friends arrived at a city in the Caucasus, where they were enrolled as members of the local opera company—Gorky as a bass, and the famous *basso profondo* as a tenor.

During his six years on Capri, from 1907 to 1913, Gorky produced an uninterrupted stream of novels, short stories, plays, critical and biographical studies. The diligent Piatnitzky sold what he could at home, while a protégé of his, a publisher called Ladishikov, poured on to the world market from Berlin anything that could not be published in Russia.

Among the Capresi who frequented the Red House was Adolfo Schiano, barber to the great, and a frequent guest at evening parties. A great performer on the guitar, Adolfo used to do a turn with a mandolin player, whose rendering of the *Serenade* of Schubert, with original variations, would have drawn tears from the very stones. A short period of service with the colours took Adolfo away from Capri for a time, and Maria

Fiodorovna was much distressed, as she was counting on him to organise a feast in honour of a friend, whose arrival on the island was anxiously awaited by the entire colony of Russian revolutionaries. This friend had suffered many persecutions in Russia and spent many years in prison, and was coming to Capri to escape the attentions of the international police, who, even outside Russia, had given him no peace, hounding him from Austria to Germany, from Germany to Denmark, from Denmark to Sweden ... where the dangerous émigré had taken part in socialist meetings and congresses.

On the evening of the party, when dinner was just beginning there was a knock at the door. Catardiello, the *factotum* of Casa Gorky, went to open it, and was surprised to see Adolfo Schiano standing before him in the uniform of a grenadier, home on a few days' leave. The lady of the house, on being told who had arrived, ran into the hall, gazed in admiration at the ferocious warrior, and had a brilliant idea.

She would get him to pretend to arrest their newly-arrived friend. Writing the name of the guest on a piece of paper she gave it to Adolfo saying, "Open this piece of paper, and read the usual formula of arrest; he won't understand anyway. But you must pronounce his name clearly like this— ". And she made him repeat the name two or three times.

Maria Fiodorovna went back into the dining-room, and going up to the guest of honour, said in a resolute voice, "It's for you—they're looking for you—the police— ".

In consternation the guest followed her out of the room.

The scene went as planned. "Are you sure it's me you're to arrest? You couldn't by any chance have made a mistake?" asked the guest.

At this Adolfo unfolded the paper he was holding

in one hand and began: "You *are* Vladimir Ilyich Ulyanov—?". But this was as far as he could get, for, unable to get his tongue round the outlandish name, he burst out laughing. Maria Fiodorovna joined in, and Vladimir Ilyich Ulyanov *alias* Nicholas Lenin, seeing the trick which had been played on him, burst out into one of those great shouts of laughter which enlivened all his stay and which are not yet forgotten on Capri.

For this special occasion Maria Fiodorovna had brought over from Sorrento the tenor Giovannino, a performer much in demand in the aristocratic villas and the big hotels of his native city, but who was appearing for the first time in the Russian colony of Capri. Giovannino, too, had a surprise in store for the guests. Towards the end of the meal he rose to his feet, and, having obtained silence, solemnly intoned in Russian an anthem which always went down very well with the guests of the Princess Gortsciakov at Sorrento: "God save the Tsar!".

Immediately there was an icy silence. Giovannino, surprised at the lack of enthusiasm, reiterated more loudly and with even greater emotion, "God save the Tsar". But suddenly his voice was drowned in a flood of cat-culls, boos and piercing wails. The Capresi musicians, immediately seized mandolins and guitars, and restored order by playing the national anthem of Naples, "Funiculì, Funiculà", in which the Russian revolutionaries joined whole-heartedly. Thus ended the first celebration at Capri in honour of Lenin.

On Capri, as at Paris and in other places in which he passed his exile, Lenin is remembered for his jovial laughter. The old fisherman Giovanni Spadaro said of it: "Only a good man could laugh like that".

Spadaro taught Lenin to fish, but said that he was a little slow on the uptake, for he could never understand when was the right moment to pull up the line—the moment, that is, when the fish takes the bait, and gives two or three tugs on the line, as if ringing a bell, to warn the fisherman. "Like this—*Drin, drin*, you see?" Spadaro would explain.

But the fish, accustomed to being caught by the Capresi, were not to be persuaded by a Russian. One day, however, Lenin had a great satisfaction; he felt two or three tugs, pulled up the line, and seeing a fine mullet wriggling in the bottom of the boat, burst into one of his merry laughs, exclaiming, "Ah, ah, *Drin, drin*".

The fishermen present joined in the laughter, and from that moment Lenin became Signor Drindrin.

From his circumspect behaviour the sailors realised that he must be a man who was suspect to the police, and when he finally left the island, Spadaro, talking to Gorky, shook his head, and said, prophetically: "Well! if the Tsar doesn't get rid of him, there's no knowing what he'll do, our Signor Drindrin".

Giovanni Spadaro never heard what happened at Ekaterinenburg.

Gorky's inability to learn a foreign language and the insensitiveness of his ear, otherwise so musical, to the sounds of the Italian language never permitted him any direct contact with the people of Capri. The conversations with fishermen, which he records, were carried on through the medium of friends. In his exchanges of ideas with people who were not Russian-speaking, it was Maria Fiodorovna who acted as interpreter.

Often the guests assembled in his house would read some composition of theirs, which would be criticised by the others. One evening the elegant poet and writer Ivan Bunin read a story set in Italy, which was well received. In his turn, Gorky, too, read a story of his called *Masaniello*; but he was not well-informed on the history and circumstances of his subject, and somebody was bold enough to criticise the language he put into the mouth of the people of Naples.

I know of only one work in which Gorky tried to give his impressions of Capri; a short story which opens with the following scene:

> The island sleeps in the austere silence; and with it sleeps the sea, as if dead. It seems as if the strange brown mass of rock, its life extinguished, had been hurled into the sea from on high, by some powerful hand.
>
> From the sea, where the golden arch of the Milky Way meets the inky waters, the island looks like some beast of legend, its hairy back arched, its monstrous face pressed down to the sea, silently lapping up the smooth and oily waters.

Among the few memories of Capri to be found in his works, is a reference to the versatility of Lenin, who was able, with equal enthusiasm, to play chess, argue for hours on end with a companion, fish, and "...walk over the rocky paths of Capri, burnt by the honest Southern sun, and admire the golden flowers of the broom and the grubby children of the fishermen". Gorky himself adored the urchins of Naples, who reminded him of the Russian street children of his own childhood wanderings, and he often wept to hear their stories; for he was as easily moved to tears, as Lenin was to laughter.

About 1907, side by side with the literary activities of Maxim Gorky, there was a great increase in Gorky's political activity, and we begin to see the first signs of that disagreement over method, if not over revolutionary principle, which characterised the relations between him and Lenin. Lenin, in the words of Gorky, "was a wonderfully perfect incarnation of will directed towards a purpose which nobody before him had dared to attempt in any practical way". Lenin felt himself chosen to put into practice the ideas of the anarchist Bakunin. The ardent Gorky maintained that the primary object of the revolution should be "the creation of conditions which permitted an increase in the cultural forces of the masses".

Capri meanwhile was assuming more and more importance as a centre of preparation and propaganda, and in 1908 it was decided to transfer there the headquarters of the Russian Socialist Party. But disagreement between the leaders prevented the idea from being carried out; and Gorky thought of something better—the setting up, in his own house, of a school in which workers could be spiritually instructed and prepared for the revolution, so that, politically educated, they would be able to take their place beside those intellectuals who were sincerely revolutionary.

An eccentric Russian millionaire, possibly Morosov, was said to have placed a huge sum of money at Gorky's disposal for the realisation of this scheme, and thus was started at the Red House (Villa Behring) the "School of Revolutionary Technique for the scientific preparation of propagandists of Russian socialism", which was the model for the "Free Association for the development and propaganda of the positive sciences" founded at Moscow after the revolution of 1917.

Capri's faculty of literature and revolution had an exceptional academic staff. Gorky and Lenin, and later Lunasciarsky, were its directors, and the teachers included the leading personalities of the party, among them the philosopher Bogdanov, Plekanov, Alexinsky, Vera Zadulich, Surguiov, Ladiznikov...

No less extraordinary were the students: workers, elementary school-teachers, and even agents of the famous *Okhrana*, the secret police of the Tsar!

For some time the school functioned amid great enthusiasm; but it failed to find favour with a scholastic inspector who was a little out of sympathy with the ideas of Gorky: a certain Joseph Dzugashvili, nick-named Zozo the Georgian, who suspected that they paid too much attention to literature at Capri, and wondered whether the teaching adhered to the ortho-dox doctrines of atheistic materialism.

The climate of the island encouraged softness, stated Zozo—and he himself was a hard man, so much so that later he changed his nickname and called him-self the Man of Steel—Stalin...

So the school of Capri was suppressed, and an at-tempt was made to start another one at San Remo.

But the seed had been sown, and was to bear fruit nine years later.

With the end of official teaching at the Red House, there began an open-air school of revolutionary tech-nique, which held its meetings by moonlight. Gorky loved the beautiful moonlit nights, and to make his en-joyment more complete used to gather round him friends and disciples who had come from Russia to hear the new gospel. These gatherings would assemble on the square in front of the little church of Sant'Andrea, at the Piccola Marina, beneath the Pensione Weber. And there, while looking forward to the advent of So-cialism, the Sun of the Future, they would wait for the rising of the sun of Capri.

The explanation of the Marxist doctrine would be followed by a short musical entertainment, and Monte Solaro would ring to famous Russian choruses and Chaliapin himself would sing.

Gradually the scene would become more animated; the guests from the nearby *pensione*, roused by the sing-ing, would come down the steep steps of the mountain to join the Russians; towards dawn the fishermen of Capri would return from the night's fishing for squids. And then we would have a real International, everyone singing without being understood—the "Volga Boat

Song" alternating with "Funiculì, Funiculà", and the "Lorelei" mingling with "Yankee Doodle".

At Capri, with the assistance of Lunasciarsky, Gorky had organised and led parties of workers, school-teachers, and young women avid of knowledge on visits to excavation sites and art galleries. When he went back to Russia, his dream realised by the revolution, he was forced to stand by while the great treasures of "bourgeois" art were destroyed.

He was forced to stand by, too, and watch the dreadful famine, the nation-wide hunger of 1919, though he had dedicated his whole work to the prevention of poverty and hardship.

His health deteriorated, and it was Lenin himself who urged him to go away. On 9 August 1921, Lenin wrote:

"...I'm tired, so tired that I can do absolutely nothing. And you who spit blood and don't go away! I assure you that it is neither conscientious nor reasonable. Here there is no possibility of being looked after, or of doing anything useful; nothing else but agitation, vain agitation. Go away, you will get better. Don't be obstinate, I implore you. Your Lenin".

This insistence, and above all the conflict of ideas and methods between him and other leaders, induced him to leave Russia and to return to Italy, where he established himself in 1922 near Sorrento.

His relations with Maria Fiodorovna had been broken off for some time. She, too, had returned to Russia, where she had been given the custody of the Crown Jewels.

In 1928 Gorky, reconciled with the Party, returned home once more. His native city was renamed after him, and he was celebrated as the greatest author of modern times.

Before leaving Italy for his own country for the last time, he felt a nostalgic longing for Capri, and came secretly to take his leave of the island from the sea, not far from the Piccola Marina.

156

Maksim Gor'kij at Villa Blaesus (1907)

August Weber (from a drawing by Mabel N. Cerio)

Chapter XI

ECCENTRICS

Capri always welcomes with joy anyone who comes to the island in search of self-expression, for such people usually end by causing as much enjoyment to others as to themselves. If they are eccentrics so much the better; it has always been the Capri way to do as one pleases.

For many years Capri gave a warm welcome to an old and fascinating Norwegian, Oscar Westergard. He used to arrive every summer, when the hot weather started; nobody could remember when these visits had begun—it seemed as though he had always been coming to the island. As soon as he reached the main square he used to look up at the sky, and as though seeing an old friend again after a long absence he would cry, "The sun, the sun, my dear, dear sun!". An old rucksack on his back, his pockets bulging with books, he would be greeted by the entire population, and would shake hands with all his old friends, inquiring about those he could not see. Since he was absolutely stone deaf, he never waited for an answer, but would continue to chatter away happily. "Tiberius, what an Emperor! and Krupp? Dead? He too? Is Hans Barth here? And where is Weber? Where is my dear friend Weber?"

August Weber, another oddity of Capri, would be sitting, lost in meditation, on the steps of the church, waiting for the excitement caused by the Norwegian's arrival to die down. As soon as things were a little calmer he would get up and go to meet Westergard, to receive a greeting similar to that which Westergard had given to the sun, only a little more vehement—"Dear, dear, dear Weber!".

Westergard used to say that he came to Capri to see his two best friends, the sun and Weber, but this was not the whole truth. Westergard had a great secret passion: the *Odyssey*. To Weber he confessed that Capri was the only place in which he could give vent to this passion, and the best spot for doing this was by the sea, under the Strandpension, near the Sirens' Rock by which Ulysses had passed on his way back to Ithaca.

So the two friends would go down to the Piccola Marina together, and there on beautiful sunny days, sitting in front of the little church of Sant'Andrea, they would amuse themselves for hours at a time. Westergard with his deep voice would shout his joy in seeing once again the sun, Capri and his friends, while Weber, without listening to him and without speaking, for he would not have been understood, would remain thoughtful and smiling, thinking up some little maxim or searching for a rhyme or an alliteration, for he used to dabble in philosophy and compose poetry.

Then one day the wind would get up, the sea would become rough, the bathers would flee, and the Sirens' Rock would become deserted. When Westergard was sure that he would not be heard by strangers, he would go down alone to the prophetic reef, take out of his pocket a copy of the *Odyssey* in the Greek text, open it at Canto XII, and in his thundering bass declaim to the sea—which surely would understand him, so imbued was it with the spirit of Hellas: "Oh most illustrious Ulysses, oh immortal glory of the Achaeans, draw near, anchor your ship and listen to our song".

Westergard's friend, August Weber, also numbered among the Capri eccentrics, is celebrated in English,

160

German, French and Italian literature as the Lunar Myth, the Philosopher of Non-sense, the Poet of Incongruity.

Having studied at the Academy of Fine Art in Munich—which he always referred to as the Athens of the Isar—he decided to seek the real land of Greece, and so began to make his way south on foot. He found that Greece, as Von Platen had remarked, began at Capri. But for all that it was only a few miles from Naples, it was not so easy to reach. On his first attempt the little boat which he had obtained to make the journey from Naples was wrecked on the shores of the Campania Felice. Setting out again, he finally reached Capri, after a voyage of three days, only to find himself arrested as a smuggler. However, like Heine at the French frontiers, he managed to convince the customs officers that the only contraband he carried was in his head, and he was allowed to land. He took possession of a little cave at the Piccola Marina, and with the help of a bricklayer turned it into a little house from which he held court like King Telon of old. He tells us in one of his many biographical pieces that his first thought was to fashion for himself a formidable army.

> My army consists
> Of twenty-six soldiers
> Strong in the wrists
> And broad in the shoulders.
> Black are their faces, black is their kit;
> You never saw army so gallant and fit.

His soldiers were of course the letters of the alphabet, with which throughout his life August Weber fought a war of liberation against good sense, logic and convention.

He began, like a good German, by evolving a philosophical system, his own private *Weltanschauung*.

Réné Descartes believed that he had solved the

problem of existence by the use of reason, expressed in the formula to end all formulas "Cogito ergo sum". At Capri August Weber went one better, and proclaimed "Cogito ergo *dumm*". With this little alteration, from Latin to German, Weber expressed his belief that all philosophy was ultimately nonsense, and dedicated his whole life to the construction of a philosophy of nonsense which kept the island amused for about half a century.

Weber was not only a philosopher; he was also a poet. The basic menu of the *table d'hôte* at the Strandpension, the little hotel he started at the Piccola Marina for artists stranded by lack of cash, was expressed in the formula: "Badate—oggi patate".

He had very great difficulty in rhyming his thoughts in Italian, but when he did succeed he was capable of great feats. The composition of the triple rhyme "Posa, osa, sposa" led him to marry a beautiful Capri girl and have a family. This relieved him from all household duties, and he was able to dedicate himself to pure philosophy, poetry and the art of being a hotelkeeper, and to ensure the happiness of his friends, his clients and all the inhabitants of Capri, whom he kept amused by his many antics.

To spread his ideas he began to wear shoes, but, be it understood, not made of leather. He possessed about a hundred pairs of shoes made of white cloth—his greatest luxury—and on these he wrote his thoughts, condensed into a few words. With these shoes he even managed to become a literary critic. When a certain novel appeared which immediately became famous but which he did not like, he wrote *Quo* on the left shoe, and *Vadis* on the right. He then appeared in the main square, whither he repaired every morning to discuss the news with his friends, sat on the steps of the church, and took off his right shoe. A critic, he implied, need not only reason with his feet, but could also express himself with his shoes.

For the clients of the Strandpension he advised, though he did not impose, a vegetarian diet, and recommended the delicious wine from his own vineyard; no chicken, he said, but good Capri rosso:

> Epargnez le sang des poussins,
> Buvez le sang des raisins.

Breakfast always consisted of a new-laid egg, on which were written a couple of lines of poetry, in which a little poetic licence was often taken to adjust the rhyme:

> Allah ist gross, und Gott ist grösser
> Jedoch mein Rotwein est famöser.

So that his pension should be suitable to all purses he charged according to the meals which his clients could afford to eat. Thus, in the *salle à manger*, after the soup and meat courses, a first exodus took place, those who paid four lire a day; after the soup, first and second courses, those who paid five, whilst the guests who paid six remained at table to eat cheese or sweet and fruit.

Weber's income came from Germany, in shining gold marks, so that he could always meet the habilities which he incurred in his hotel. To his great surprise the Strandpension attracted many foreigners, and business prospered. Weber was unaccustomed to this sort of thing, and wondered whether he could stand the strain, but fortunately it was just then that he met an artist of quite exceptional character, the only woman worthy of mention amongst the great eccentrics of Capri, Lucy Flannigan, an American.

She came from the Boston Art School, and she

soon fell under the spell of the French impressionists, whose influence was very strong at that time in America. Having won a travelling scholarship, she set out for Paris to study under Claude Monet, to whom she had been recommended.

Her ship brought her to Naples, and from there she decided to pay a visit to Capri. At the Piccola Marina, where she had gone for a swim, she met August Weber. He invited her to have lunch at the Strandpension, and she was so enchanted with the place that she remained there for the rest of her life.

At the end of six months she had spent all that remained of the first instalment of her scholarship, and as she had not put in an appearance at Paris the award was discontinued. However, Weber offered to open an account for her at the hotel—an account which was to be paid by the proceeds from the sale of her impressionistic paintings of Capri. These pictures certainly made a great impression on their admirers, but unfortunately nobody bought them. At that time Capri was always painted in blue tones—ultramarine for the sea, cobalt blue for the sky, and ash blue for the rocks. Miss Flannigan, as though affected by colour blindness, began to paint everything red. She became the tormented soul of the landscape of Capri, and she used an enormous quantity of very expensive paints, such as vermilion, burnt siena, and all sorts and qualities of varnish, all of which were charged to the hotel account.

In the end she amassed so many pictures that they would not all fit into her room, and a meeting of patrons decided by a large majority that they could no longer tolerate Miss Flannigan at the hotel. Weber, finding himself in a minority of one, suggested that they should continue to keep the prolific painter at the hotel with simple board and lodging, but should rent her a large room in the outhouses, still known today as the Studio of the Piccola Marina, and make it an annexe of the Strandpension. Since, after all, he was the proprietor, Weber's proposal was accepted. From that time dates the really great period of Lucy Flannigan's artistic activity, which lasted from the beginning of the century until 1935, when she died in Rome after a serious operation, having outlived her patron by seven years.

Being a good hotel-keeper Weber faithfully kept the account of his unusual guest, binding the records into volumes year by year until their number equalled those of the *Encyclopaedia Britannica*. Following the style of the old German almanachs, Lucy Flannigan's accounts were interpolated with little stories, verses and anecdotes, and decorated with many little drawings in black and white, or sometimes in colour. The first volume, dated 1902, ended with a puzzle, never solved:

> Wer weiss ob, dann und wann,
> Bezahlt Miss Flannigan?

Among the more exotic crazes which have swept the fashionable world of Capri must be recorded that of having one's portrait painted in Chinese style by a charming painter from Saigon, Lé-van-Dé, who paid frequent visits to the island over a period of years. This interesting artist, who based his art on the Chinese "professional" painters—a group of modernistic revolutionaries for whom art was no longer a gentlemanly occupation to while away one's leisure hours—was a follower of the movement led by King-kung-pah. This reviver of Far Eastern art taught his followers to graft the experience and technique of western painting on to the old tree of Chinese art, and urged them to study in Europe. Lé-van-Dé had distinguished himself in his native Indo-China, and was encouraged to further his studies in France.

But Lé-van-Dé also amused himself with the art of

tattooing—an activity which was to cause him much discomfort. In his time there appeared on the island some very distinguished Indians, amongst them Chandra Bose, the Communist agitator, and a certain Prince Tagore, a nephew of Sir Rabindranath, both of whom, like all other respectable visitors, aroused the suspicions of the Fascist Government. The police were given orders to keep them under observation, but an over-zealous police officer, burning to distinguish himself in some way, let them escape and naturally fell into disgrace. To make amends for his failure he begait to watch Lé-van-Dé and surprised him one day when he was tattooing a bather's arm. A mere glance from a distance was enough for him to recognise the dreaded sign of the hammer and sickle on the girl's arm. This was only to be expected, for in China Communist cells were on the increase, and it must be much the same in Indo-China. And Lé-van-Dé came from Indo-China.

When the discovery was reported to Rome, the order was given to arrest the suspected painter, to take him to Naples, and from there to send him on to Rome. It was the first Communist plot to be discovered in Capri, and one can imagine the excitement at the police station. And so Lé-van-Dé finished up at the Regina Coeli prison, was then summoned before a special tribunal and waited to hear his fate.

Meanwhile on Capri the local magistrate received instructions to examine the arm of the tattooed bather. Imagine his chagrin to find, not the sinister emblem of the red peril, but the unmistakable and universal sign of eternal love: a heart pierced by an arrow! And thus Lé-van-Dé escaped the firing squad.

C.C. Coleman (portrait by Rose O'Neill)

Axel Munthe on the chapel terrace at San Michele with his arms
full of animal protégés (a monkey and the fox-terrier Léonie)

CHAPTER XII

VOLUNTARY EXILES

Among the many people who, coming from distant
lands, made Capri their home during the nineteenth
century was Henry Wreford, the *doyen* of the English
colony and for fifty years a resident on the island. Wreford came to Capri for a day and stayed for half a century. He arrived as a special correspondent of *The
Times* in 1842, and the last of his articles in that paper
appeared on 22 March 1892. He died four days later in
his home, Villa Croce.

From Capri, Wreford conducted a vigorous campaign, as correspondent and political observer, in support of the Italian struggle for independence. It was he
who raised, in letters to Gladstone and Lord Palmerston, the question of the Italian patriots, and especially
those of Naples, who had been subjected to cruel re-
pressions and imprisonment by the tyrannical absolut-
ism of the Bourbons. In 1850, Palmerston sent William
Gladstone on a secret mission to Naples to meet Wreford, who gave him detailed information about the hor-
rible conditions of the political prisoners in Naples.
This prompted Gladstone to write his famous open letter to Lord Palmerston, in which the anti-liberal régime
of the Bourbons was described as a "negation of God
erected into a system of government".

The propaganda begun by Henry Wreford in *The
Times* and carried on from Capri in his correspondence

169

was one of the factors which brought about Queen Victoria's change of attitude towards the Italian revolutionaries, whom she began to regard with more favour. In this way was born the "traditional friendship" between Italy and England, so dear to the Italian liberals as to become the pivot of external politics for almost a century.

At Villa Croce, and later in his other house, Villa Cesina, Wreford kept, together with relics of the Italian wars of independence which he followed as correspondent of *The Times*, the correspondence which he had with Victor Emmanuel II, Cavour, Crispi, Garibaldi and other patriots, and with the group of Neapolitan patriots in whom he had taken an interest during their imprisonment.

Writing to *The Times* from Capri on 18 September 1860, he deplored the part played by Alexandre Dumas in the affairs of Naples, stigmatising his arrogant and boastful ways, and asking how he had managed to attach himself so firmly to Garibaldi. He went on to describe Dumas as "a celebrated novelist whose personal adventures would appear fictitious if he himself did not guarantee their authenticity".

Like his friend Gladstone, Wreford was a most cultured man and an excellent Latin scholar; and on Capri he did much praiseworthy work for local education. Like other Englishmen before him, he did not ignore the island's attractions; he had two beautiful villas, many friends, and always kept an excellent table—in short, he identified himself so much with the life of Capri that he never thought of reconciling himself with the life of England.

Another voluntary exile who made Capri his home during the second half of the nineteenth century was Colonel J.C. Mac Kowen, a gentleman planter from Louisiana. Having fought with General Lee during the American Civil War and disapproving of the emancipation of the slaves, he sold his estates on the termination of hostilities, and in 1866 came to Europe. He studied in Germany where he qualified as a doctor, and in 1876 came to Capri. After a few years he bought a large estate at Damecuta, with the secret hope of growing cotton, or at least Indian corn. Despite his authoritarian ways, his arrogant scowl, his boots, and his spurs, which made him a perfect example of a slave-owner, Mac Kowen lavished his professional care on the poor, and kept them supplied with medicines. At the same time, to preserve the character of the Southern planter, he gave them the rough edge of his tongue. In Anacapri he was known as *Sciacca e medica*—strike and heal.

In 1882, while carrying out some land improvement schemes on his Damecuta estate, he realised that it lay directly over the Blue Grotto. Claiming that the Grotto belonged to him, he gave up his plantation idea and began to arrange for the construction of a tunnel, which would allow him to conduct tourists to the Grotto by land, thus sparing them the discomforts of the sea trip, and incidentally doing himself a good turn.

The entire population of the island was horrified at the possible consequences of this action, and rose up in revolt, starting a lawsuit which went on for a couple of years. Displaying great erudition in Roman Law, the Colonel maintained that his rights over the land extended *usque ad inferos*, and therefore included the Grotto. In the end, however, the island triumphed. The excavation of the tunnel was abandoned before it had got properly started, and, since the diggings had brought to light the remains of one of Augustus' villas, the Colonel, already a good historian and classical scholar, decided to devote himself to archaeology.

About this time interest in the classical antiquities of Capri was becoming widespread among the residents of the island. They wished to acquire archaeological remains with which to ornament their villas. The increasing demand was met by an increasing supply, for when the local genuine articles were not available large-scale imitations could easily be procured from the workshops of Naples.

While Mac Kowen was making his first excavations at Damecuta in 1884, Axel Munthe arrived on Capri, and began a similar search for antiquities in Anacapri with which to decorate his Ville San Michele, and rivalry grew up between the two.

In the meantime Mac Kowen, now married and established in his red house, turreted and battlemented like the blockhouse of a Louisiana plantation, went on digging and collecting pieces of marble and terracotta, which he stuck up on the façade and courtyard of his home. One morning, one of his spies told him that a farmer digging in his fields had uncovered an ancient tomb between the flats of Damecuta and the high ground round Tiberino. The Colonel hurried to the spot, only to find that he had been forestalled by Axel Munthe, who was bending over the excavation, turning over in his hands the ancient objects which were being brought to light. Uncovering the tomb, Munthe extracted a double tile, which slipped from his hand, fell to the ground and broke.

"Barbarian!" shouted Mac Kowen in a sudden access of rage.

"Slave-driver!" retorted Munthe, with Scandinavian calm.

This epithet must have given the Colonel an idea, for he approached the tomb, examined it carefully and announced with an authoritative air: "A poor burial! Not even the dish with food for the after-life, which even freedmen were given! It must be the tomb of a slave, perhaps one of the many brought in from Acarnania by Augustus' architects to clear the land on which the villa of Damecuta was built. We must have a closer

172

look; I wonder if there's a coin between the jaws; let's see if we can find the skull...".

He was stretching out his hand to rummage in the pile of bones heaped up on the floor of the tomb, when Dr Munthe broke in in warning tones: "For your information, the bones are mine, and woe betide anyone who touches them! And even if the tomb is poor, it might belong to someone of noble origin. If only you knew your history! Anyway, I've bought the whole thing".

The owner of the farm, who had been present at this little scene, confirmed that the Swedish doctor had in fact bought the whole excavation. Dr Munthe had begun about this time to rebuild the ruined fabric of San Michele, and in anticipation of its future layout, was trying to get hold of all the mortal remains which he could find. In due course, the foundations of the now famous Villa of San Michele harboured a collection of the most distinguished bones of the Imperial epoch which the island could yield.

The discovery of the tomb of uncertain origin widened the rift between the American and the Swede. Mac Kowen, mindful of the glories of slavery in its golden age under the Greeks, resolutely maintained that the tomb was of the period of Augustus, well known for his Hellenistic tastes. Munthe, on the other hand, favoured Tiberius, and considered the remains found in the tomb to be those of a Roman matron, probably of Imperial blood, who had died at Anacapri and been buried in a humble grave. The controversy, bitter from its very start, soon developed into a fierce quarrel, involving by degrees all the notables of the foreign colony, and ended by producing the first great schism among the foreign residents of Capri.

The Anglo-Saxons, famed for their hatred of slavery and love of animals, sided in a body with Munthe, who had already made his mark with his first effort in the literary field, "The Dogs of Capri", published in *Blackwood's Magazine*. The Americans, too, took Munthe's side, especially the Yankees, who were glad to be able to their own back on the Colonel for the way he was always nagging them about emancipation, and how it was ruining the South. From archaeological differences the two opponents soon passed to personal insults, and before long Capri had to record a memorable challenge to a duel. Happily, the duel never got very far, because of a difference over the choice of weapons, which Mac Kowen claimed as his right, although it really rested with Munthe, as the challenged party. The Colonel insisted on pistols—two for each dueller, according to the practice of the landed aristocracy of Louisiana in such matters. Munthe, on the other hand, with the support of the predominantly Victorian Anglo-Saxon opinion on the island, maintained that for his arrogance and overbearing manner, the ex-slave-owner, should be publicly horsewhipped. And so, from then on, Mac Kowen and Munthe went about prepared for all eventualities, the one with his pockets bulging with a couple of barely concealed duelling pistols, the other openly and threateningly brandishing a horse-whip; and whenever they saw one another coming, they would glare at each other from a safe distance.

The rivalry continued and the breach between the two men was never healed. Mac Kowen watched the building of the Villa San Michele, and the accumulation there of the island's rarest treasures. Finally he decided. He began to pack up his papers, the manuscripts in which were contained the fruits of his long researches; he took down from the walls of his house some of the authentic pieces of his collection. He left behind, however, in the courtyard of his villa, the rare mutilated pieces of marble excavated at Damecuta, the valuable terracottas, and the fragments contaning his most important inscriptions. And one summer's morning in

174

1902, ignoring the horrors of emancipation, and the disgrace of the Union, which humiliated his homeland, he took ship at Naples for New Orleans.

Two weeks later, he stepped ashore in his native city, went into a bar in the port, ordered a high-ball, and began to talk to one of his fellow-townsmen. As luck would have it, he struck an abolitionist, who began to sing the praises of emancipation...

John Clay Mac Kowen suddeuly felt a return of his old ideals, a rekindling of his former love for his birthplace, and turning on his companion, he began to abuse him for his opinions. The latter, without wasting any words, pulled out of his pocket a handsome old Southern pistol, and shot Mac Kowen dead.

Of all the painters who have lived on Capri the most memorable personality was Charles Caryl Coleman, the much-loved Uncle Charlie of the island's foreign colony at the beginning of the century.

Having come to Italy from America at an early age to study painting, Coleman was filled with enthusiasm for the heroic deeds of the *Risorgimento*, and meeting Garibaldi, decided to enlist under his command. But the call of his own country, threatened by the secession of the South, prevented this plan, and the would-be Garibaldian re-crossed the Atlantic.

In 1864 he came back to Italy and, renouncing further studies, set up as a painter in Venice, with a studio near the Torre dell'Orologio, which was frequented by the most celebrated artists of the time. Later he moved to Rome, sharing a studio in the Piazza di Spagna with Elihu Vedder, who had made his name with the illustrations for the *Rubaiyat*. Finally he came and settled on Capri, where by the beginning of this century he had achieved the dignified position of *doyen* of the foreign artists in Italy.

Studio is hardly the right word for the scenes of

Coleman's activities. His various *ateliers* were work-shops, picture factories specialising in the production, in turn romantic, classical, popular, or even simply commercial, of scenes of the Italian countryside. The bulk of his work was exported to America, but some was also sold at the annual exhibitions of the Royal Academy and the Salon. He had many buyers and admirers, and it was for this public, rather than for himself, that Coleman created his extraordinary dwelling—an essential background to the painter-antiquarian, of which he was without any doubt the best-known and most-honoured example.

Coleman, now hardly remembered in America (where in their time his works had had scores of admirers and purchasers), and completely forgotten in Europe, achieved fame by the clever choice of a sentimental motif set in the beautiful scenery of Capri, whose trees he loved. Acquiring what had formerly been the guesthouse of Madre Serafina's convent, he restored it in the most excruciating taste, and would show his friends and admirers, photographs of this artistic dwelling, in which he appeared posing under the pergolas in the garb of his trade; and with visible signs of emotion, he would explain: " I originally bought the house just to save a magnificent tree which grew in the cloisters, the most beautiful tree in the island, possibly in the whole of Italy, an oleander planted by a Saint... ".

Unfortunately this oleander had begun its life at least two centuries after the death of Madre Serafina.

In the first years of Coleman's residence, the house had been subjected to a dose of the Baroque, as befitted the repository of the traditions of the Venerabie Madre Serafina. But at the beginning of the century the Oriental vogue made a belated arrival on Capri, and Coleman, to tone in his abode with the pictures it would have to inspire, superimposed on it a Moorish interior of *harem* style. Thus transformed, the House of the Oleander became the first, and the ugliest, example of that Moorish architecture from which was concocted the non-existent "Capri style".

But the taste of the time changed again, and Coleman was not slow to follow suit. Convinced that a painter should be inspired by his surroundings, he applied himself to the task of redecorating the House of the Oleander, swamping it under a mass of medieval battlements, turrets, arches, buttresses, gargoyles and gutters, all designed to create an atmosphere of the purest romanticism.

These, however, were but stages in the art of C.C. Coleman, which was destined to reach its climax only when the artist had received the revelation of the classical world which existed all around him. In no time at all the House of the Oleander took on a new aspect, with *triclinium, impluvium, atrium* and Pompeian portico, its walls encrusted with bas-reliefs and inscriptions, its terraces cluttered up with mutilated statues, broken columns, open sarcophagi and empty funerary urns. Attired in this prevalently Greco-Roman dress, it changed its name and became Villa Narcissus.

Coleman's classical painting did not have the success it deserved. It arrived too late, when all the circuses, *triclinia* and baths of ancient Rome had been exploited and sentimentalised by Alma Tadema. His *Tiberian Orgy*, intended for the Library of the Senate in Washington, hardly caused a stir; and his usually faithful public remained unconvinced by *A girl of the time of Tiberius*. The classical *genre* had lost its appeal.

Meanwhile, a whole stack of art treasures had accumulated at Villa Narcissus—statues, lecterns, missals, manuscripts, stoles, thuribles... Its rooms, dark, dusty, never open to the sun, were suffocating. The sumptuous "private chapel" of the painter smelt of the sacristy; while amidst the hotch-potch of religious furnishings, a genuine masterpiece, *Saint Elizabeth of Hungary*,

177

by an unknown craftsman of Nuremberg, slowly decayed.

At this point Coleman felt the need for a breath of fresh air, and decided to open the double-arched window which gave on to the Bay of Naples. As his eye travelled over the scene, his glance fell on Vesuvius. In a flash he saw the immense possibilities of the mountain; and from that moment, we can say, he changed, for the last time, his manner, his style and his subject. He began to paint exclusively the faithful volcano, in all its poses, and in all its many moods. From then on Coleman's biography and the history of Vesuvius were one and the same thing. Every exhibition of his made a new contribution to the already rich iconography of the fiery mountain; eruptions and exhibitions followed one another in ceaseless alternation.

The new *genre* was a great, indeed an enormous success. An ordinary Vesuvius with a conventional plume of smoke and an Italian pine in the foreground fetched as much as 100 dollars; and the famous picture of the volcano in winter, with its summit covered in snow, as seen through the double window of Villa Narcissus, with almond blossom in a figured bowl on the windowsill, reached twice that figure.

Having established an exclusive right to the subject, Coleman found himself on a wave of prosperity; and it would have lasted indefinitely had it not been for the eruption of 1906. This was a real disaster, for apart from destroying part of the village of Ottaiano, it completely ruined Coleman's painting by altering the profile of the mountain, and shattering its classical cone.

Coleman, the man of the great eruptions, the depicter of the volcano with the conventional but perfect form, could not, and would not, bring himself to accept a compromise—paint a Vesuvius now almost lifeless, surmounted only by lazy, uncertain wisps of white smoke: depict the shattered outline... Nor was he young

178

enough to wait while the cone built itself up again, and the mountain reassumed its former aspect.

Having no wish to come to terms with the situation, he gave up painting; and this was perhaps his real and his greatest fortune. For if in the years of his most intense activity, he had enjoyed a certain fame, he had not been able to escape the charge of being a contemporary. But now, thrown up, as it were, on the beach of time, and practising the most rigorous artistic abstinence, he began gradually to come into his own, and to acquire the reputation of having been one of the great painters of the nineteenth century. As he grew older, the sculptural lines of his handsome face became more pronounced; and with his prophetic white beard and his flowing locks, set off by a characteristic black beret, he would have passed, in the last years of his life, for a reproduction in wax of Michelangelo, had it not been for the fact that he resembled even more that sculptor's statue of Moses. He died in 1928 at the age of 87.

Coleman knew and entertained in his studio some of the greatest painters of the nineteenth century—Sargent, Leighton, Speed, Woodhouse—a whole procession of chosen spirits who visited Capri, and of whose stay there remains a trace in the visitors' book of Villa Narcissus.

Norman Douglas

CHAPTER XIII

COLLECTORS' PIECE

FROM the *Story of San Michele*, everyone is familiar with Axel Munthe's Villa San Michele. It was an example of what could be done with the "antiquarian villa", which for more than a century had enraptured the foreigners who came to seek treasures of ancient art on Capri, where all visible signs of the flourishing Greek colony and of the imposing home of the Caesars had vanished. But San Michele was created for the public, was intended to be an attraction for tourists. For Munthe himself, and for a handful of fortunate friends and admirers, there was the Torre Materita, where Munthe really lived and where he had assembled a small but exquisite collection of ancient treasures.

The most precious jewel of this collection was the mask of Parian marble, thought to be the image of an oracle. Munthe did not himself claim that it was an original work of Phidias and, as such, the only example of the great Athenian sculptor's work to have come down to us. He did not readily show this marble, but always ended up by making an exception. There was much beating about the bush before you got there. After having shown you the most important items in his collection, he would remember that you had not yet seen the "Prince"—a perfectly preserved skeleton of a small child, which stood under a glass cover on the sideboard in the dining-room. Passing with the visitor into

181

a corridor, Munthe would approach a small table covered with a crimson velvet cloth, and seizing an end, would pull the cloth away with a sudden jerk to reveal the marvel—the Oracle: a mask of white marble, crystalline and lightly gilded. The eye-sockets were empty, and the lips, curved round the opening of the mouth, were compressed in a spasm of pain, or perhaps traversed by a quiver of joy. It seemed that the Oracle was about to speak; you could almost hear the still voice issuing from the void behind the empty mouth. But it was perhaps Munthe himself who created this illusion, for, throwing the velvet cloth back on top of the mask, he would invariably ask: " Did you hear? ". Then, without giving you time to answer, as if afraid of the revelation at which he had hinted, he would say, alluding to the sculpture. " School of Phidias ".

He never said—he never had said: " By Phidias ", because he was not, or pretended that he was not, sure. But it was this very uncertainty of his which caused the sculpture to be considered original, for if there had been any doubt about the authenticity of the work, Munthe would certainly have claimed it as genuine. The hypothesis was strengthened by the stout chain which secured the mask to the corridor's massive wall. Even more persuasive were the circumstances in which the celebrated mask was found. Many years previously, Munthe had uncovered the marble while digging up the land around the Torre to transplant some cypresses which he had removed from Villa Falconieri. After a little polishing, it betrayed to his expert eyes unmistakable signs of Periclean workmanship. But, in some doubt as to whether it might not be one of the many copies of Greek sculptures brought to Capri to enrich the collections of Augustus, he decided to call in the expert, Salomon Reinach. On examining the marble, the expert declared it to be of Phidian workmanship and almost certainly original; moreover, he provided a theory to explain its presence on Capri. Although they had never colonised the island, the Phoenicians, or "Semites of the Sea"—as Reinach called them, and like himself, seafaring archaeologists—certainly established there a trading station, which they used as a naval base, or, more probably, as a dump for the booty obtained on their piratical expeditions.

But the rich colonists and wealthy merchants of Crete, Athens and Sparta, though they might route their ships far from the Faraglioni, nevertheless had to round the western promontory of Capri to reach Cumae. It only needed a south-westerly gale for their ships to be hurled on to the rocks of Materita; so that it is certainly possible that the famous marble which we now call the Oracle of Phidias, which vanished from Greece, and of which Pausanias lamented the disappearance, should eventually have found its way to Capri...

Having formulated this hypothesis, Salomon Reinach thought no more about the subject; but it came back to him many years later, when he was taking Pierpont Morgan, the great American financier and patron of the arts, around the Louvre. Morgan had just returned from a fruitless visit to the Middle East in search of Greek masterpieces with which to enrich the museums of America; and entering the room where Greek sculptures were displayed, he stopped in ecstasy in front of a piece of the Parthenon frieze, and asked anxiously: "We can at least be sure of this one, can't we: this *is* by Phidias?". Morgan had decided to find and purchase a work of Phidias at any cost. But in London, Rome, Athens, wherever he came across works attributed to Phidias, doubts of their complete authenticity rose to torment him.

So he was very disappointed when Reinach said, pointing to the famous frieze, "Certainly, the sculpture is in the best style, and without any doubt in the manner of Phidias, perhaps directly inspired by the master himself, but the actual work could be by a pupil of his, or a group of his pupils working together. As far as we know, all Phidias' works have disappeared without leaving any trace except the fame they won for their creator; the gold and ivory statues from the Parthenon, the bas-reliefs of the Temple of Zeus... you would not find an original in Paris or Athens or Rome".

Thwarted and unconvinced, the financier insisted, in the tone of one not to be gainsaid, "I simply must get a work of Phidias for the Metropolitan Museum".

It was then that Reinach suddenly remembered Munthe's discovery. "In that case", he said, "you can't do better than to go to Capri", and he told the story of Munthe's lucky find.

Morgan decided to take his advice, and would have left at once, had not the news of the 1907 Wall Street disaster reached him the next day, and he returned to America.

Two months later he left New York to attend a meeting of bankers in Rome in early January. He arrived in Naples on Sunday; the meeting in Rome was fixed for Monday, so that he had one day free for the trip that should have seen the fulfilment of his most ardent longings.

At that time the port of Capri had not been built, and since a fresh north-east wind had been blowing through the previous night, backing in the morning to the north, the crossing from Naples was very rough and the disembarkation into small rowing boats a somewhat lively operation. However Morgan took no notice. He had often crossed the Atlantic in gales and cyclones which made the north wind seem by comparison a trifle.

Once on land Morgan decided to enjoy the trip to the full, and in order to stretch his cramped legs after ten days at sea he preferred to climb up to the village on foot by the old steps, delighting at each twist which brought a new enchantment into view.

When he arrived in the village square he leant out over the colonnaded terrace, in ecstasies at the wonderful scene. The sky, swept by the increasingly strong wind, had become an unbelievably clear blue; the Bay of Naples was like a great bowl, rimmed with sapphire, in which the sea, coloured like lapis-lazuli, danced and gleamed in the sun, while, last and greatest marvel, Vesuvius, chilled by the north wind, was covered by a mantle of snow.

Breathing the fresh sparkling air was like sipping champagne. Morgan, carried away by the pleasant sensation caused by the enjoyment of this enchanting panorama, had to tear his eyes away from it to go to the nearby hotel. When the porter saw him enter the hall with no luggage he immediately assumed a haughty look, and mentally classified him as one of those passing travellers who came to Capri for a day trip.

However, the financier was unmoved by the contempt of the head porter, and going up to him asked for news of Munthe.

"Axel?" the porter asked, as haughty as ever.

"Yes, Axel Munthe."

"Egypt."

"Isn't he at Materita?"

"No, he's in the Valley of the Kings."

After this show of superiority the proud concierge unbent a little and explained what had happened. Dr Munthe, who had not practised his ordinary profession for years had been called a few days earlier to the bedside of an, as yet, unidentified Pharaoh.

Morgan was very put out by this news, but did not put off his planned visit. "Can I at least get into the Torre and see the Oracle?"

Out of the question: the Torre was shut and the property was enclosed by high walls and guarded by

185

fierce watchdogs. "Quite impossible to see it", the porter assured him, and then becoming more friendly he added, "Anyway it's not worth your while...".

"Why? Isn't it a genuine Phidias?"

"A copy!"

"But a Roman or Augustan copy perhaps?"

"Yes"—a smile—"Roman from the Via del Babuino!".

At that moment a gong sounded and the porter announced, as if to close the conversation, "Lunch is served".

"What a strange and interesting island", thought Pierpont Morgan, as he lingered at table after a very satisfying meal. "Why should I go at four, there must be other boats, at six or at eight. Certainly every two hours."

If he left at eight he would be in time to catch the last train to Rome from Naples.

A doubt assailed him. Supposing there was not another later boat. In Europe things were never as one wanted.

The very thought of not leaving that day appalled him. What would Baring and Morgenstern and the Director of the Crédit Lyonnais think of him?

He shook himself free of the feeling of drowsy well-being induced by the wine and the over-copious *pasta*, paid his bill and left the dining-room.

In the hall he looked at his watch—just two o'clock. He turned to the porter and asked him what he could do to pass the time till the boat left.

"Which boat?"

By now the provocative manner of this over-dressed flunkey had begun to annoy him.

"You mean there are lots of boats, I suppose, one leaving every quarter of an hour."

"No more are leaving."

"What about the four o'clock steamer?"

186

"It left at two."

"I don't understand; explain yourself."

By way of reply the porter pointed heavenwards out of the large hall window and cupped his hand to his ear. The American was nonplussed by this mimicry. "Can't you hear?" said the porter. "Don't you see what's going on outside?"

Outside the wind was howling, its strength revealed by the whirlwinds of dead leaves spinning past the window.

"Don't you see", insisted the porter, "*È scesa la tramontana*—the north wind's here!".

Quite impervious to the news of this portentous event, Morgan explained, "I'm talking about the four o'clock steamer".

"When that north wind gets up", explained the porter in his turn, "the boat leaves at two, or at one o'clock. It goes to shelter in a nearby harbour".

"What a country, Europe!"

"Here, dear sir, we are in Capri, and Europe has nothing to do with it."

After this proud outburst the porter became more communicative. "You perhaps don't know of the *tramontana* and that explains everything; you don't understand it. The north wind is a woman, the only woman among all the winds, and she is a fury. When she begins as she has done today it's like the end of the world in the Bay. All around Capri traffic comes to a standstill; the boats can't get near the steamer, anchors don't hold, chains give way. Then the steamer thinks, 'What am I doing here?'. It gives two or three blasts on its siren, out of formality, pretending to warn the passengers, who naturally have no time to embark, it weighs anchor and steers for Ischia or Baia or Castellammare, according to its captain. All the captains are local men from the coast nearby, and each one makes for his own village".

Pierpont Morgan, far from being moved by this, grew more annoyed and asked sharply, "When is the next steamer going to leave?".

The porter was by now well into his story; he had a weakness for the *tramontana*. "When will it leave? Who knows? In the good old days the *tramontana* used to last for three days. One could rely on it. One stayed three days, even four, waiting for the rage of the north-east wind with which it finishes, without any communication with the mainland. But now everything is changed; sometimes after two days, even twenty-four hours the wind goes to the bad and we lose the visitors, who take advantage of the lull to leave."

Morgan had stopped listening. "I", he thundered in no uncertain tone, "I absolutely must leave today".

"Impossible."

"At all costs, I must get to Rome."

"And how are you going to do it?"

Exasperated a moment previously by the unexpected misfortune and almost infuriated by the porter's insolence, the great American financier suddenly became calm and impassive, realising that he had not been recognised, and announced, "I am Morgan".

Seeing that the porter, who remained even more impassive than himself, did not understand, or pretended not to understand, he expanded his statement: "I am Pierpont Morgan ... of the Steel Corporation".

"What can I do about it? It doesn't make any difference about your leaving."

"But in America..."

"America is one thing, Capri is another; take advantage of the fact that you are now in Capri..."

But he never finished his sentence, for the indignant American turned on his heel and went out. Once in the street Morgan, struck by the full force of the wind, began to understand what the *tramontana* really meant. Right opposite the Palace Hotel he saw the shining windows of the Tourist Office, and he stopped to admire the striting relief map on which was shown how, following an arrow that left every capital of Europe and America, one might reach Capri and (thought Morgan) also leave the place, if only the *tramontana* were not blowing. Then, as he wanted information, he went into the office.

The two clerks, quickly guessing the situation when they saw him, had the pleasant feeling that the sight of every stranger gives when he can't leave the island. One of them ran through the meteorological report, going over in his mind the most pleasant features of the island's climate. The other, a devotee of statistics, began to shuffle through the list of the non-Catholic cemetery, hoping to persuade the newcomer to buy a grave, since he maintained that strangers should stay in Capri for ever.

Morgan got down to business straight away. "I have to leave."

The two clerks looked at each other amazed.

"Leave?" asked one incredulously, and the other repeated it as if he hadn't understood. "Leave?"

The scene was a frequent one in the Tourist Office, and they acted it very naturally. Morgan, however, took no notice and continued, "I simply must leave. It's impossible? I know, the porter at the Palace has already explained—please don't repeat it all to me: the *tramontana*, the steamer's siren... You must find me some means to leave".

"But there isn't one."

"Never mind, you must find one. I don't mind the expense."

"Well, if it's like that, there is a way", admitted one of the clerks; "there's the rowing boat of Coccolillo, a sailor well known in these parts. Only Coccolillo could work the miracle... if he would take the risk, but

189

will he? Of course, it would cost you quite a bit. Shall we try?".

Before Morgan had time to reply he took up the telephone, rang, hit the instrument, shouted for the marine office and waited, stamping his feet. He shouted so much that in the end he got Coccolillo himself on the line and explained the situation to him.

"Hullo, hullo... do you understand? Impossible? Not even to Sorrento? Yes, Sorrento... prepared to pay... just a moment."

He interrupted the conversation, consulted the American and returned to the receiver. "Hullo, to Sorrento, or any other place on the coast, as long as he gets to the mainland... and the price... eight hundred? Isn't that a bit steep?"

He spoke to Morgan in English. "He's asking a lot, but he's using a unique boat, a well-known one on the coast; it used to be a rival to the steamer and brought the mail over in any weather; if it seems too much..."

"But how much does he want?" asked Morgan impatiently.

"...and the tip, two or three hundred more, depends on your kindness. Can I settle it, and for when?"

"I must catch the express at eight o'clock."

"Well, allowing two hours at the most for the crossing and one and a half for the car to Naples, shall we fix the time for four o'clock?"

He returned to the telephone and confirmed conditions for the hiring, a thousand lire, but about the time of departure Coccolillo could not agree. The *tramontana* was getting more and more violent and might back to the west. The sailors wanted to be sure of reaching the coast of Sorrento before nightfall; it was better to be earlier.

When the arrangements were finished the clerk explained: "We've fixed the departure for half-past three. That leaves you more than an hour. What would you

190

like to do? I would suggest taking a carriage and going down to the shore by the carriage road. You would get a marvellous view".

"Excellent", agreed Morgan.

"I advise you to stop at the Two Gulfs, that has an unequalled view, and a bit farther on, stop at the non-Catholic cemetery, and look at the new part: it's all planted with orange-trees; you should go to a funeral there in springtime, what a scent! Do you know the song 'Connais tu le pays'?"

"Thank you, said Morgan, "I promise to follow your advice", and off he went.

Fate willed that on that day the destinies of two men were to meet. Two men as different as Pierpont Morgan, then a world-famous financier, and Hans Paule, who is still famous on Capri. The two destinies clashed because Morgan had to go to Rome to found a bank, and Paule to Positano to paint a picture. The German artist, unaware that the steamer had already left, came down by the funicular at three-thirty. Having learnt on the way down of the boat's early departure, he was pleasantly surprised on reaching the shore to hear a sailor calling him: "To Sorrento, *signore?* The rowing-boat is ready... you must hurry!".

Paule followed him, running. When he reached the quay he could see the sailors were very eager to be off, but wanting to make sure of their destination he asked "To Sorrento?".

"Yes, Sorrento", shouted the boat's mate impatiently, "come aboard, can't you see what a storm is coming up?".

Paule threw his bag to a sailor, leapt in and sat himself down in the prow.

"Away there!" ordered the mate. The boat pulled away from the quay, and driven by the vigorous ardour of the rowers sped out to sea, its sharp prow cutting through the breakers that rose against it.

191

Pierpont Morgan had asked his driver to go slower so that he might enjoy to the full the beautiful drive. All the same he arrived in time to see Coccolillo's famous rowing-boat pass the end of the mole and disappear in the direction of Sorrento.

Oil-mil in Anacapri

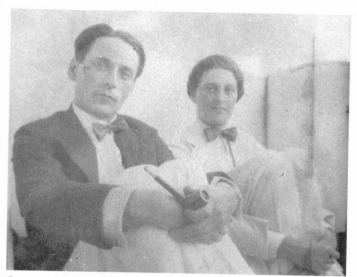

Compton Mackenzie and Mimì Franchetti

Curzio Malaparte and Raffaele Castello

193

Marchesa Casati Stampa

Chapter XIV

THE SHOW GOES ON

During the last war, the colourful life of the inhabitants of Capri could no longer continue.

Capri, by nature an international island, has always avoided getting involved in nationwide conflagrations, and has remained *au-dessus de la purée*. But I, personally, had not remained neutral: in the event of a serious threat to the island, I had promised an American lady to intervene.

This lady was the owner of a beautiful villa, and had turned her garden into a bird sanctuary, a real artificial paradise for birds. In the middle was an immense aviary, for birds from hot and humid climes, with running hot and cold water, central heating and other tropical comforts, while ranged around were large cages for other species from sub-tropical and temperate zones. In this paradise, with its delightful living conditions, as removed as possible from those of nature, the birds lived and died happily, enjoying an artificial life and a natural death.

While the lady was still living on Capri, birds that died were replaced by purchases made in Naples, New York, Hamburg and Paris. But when war broke out in 1940, and she was forced to leave, she made me promise faithfully that in the event of a serious threat to the island, I would painlessly consign to the next world all the surviving birds, thus sparing them the horrors of shelling and bombing, of high explosives, phosphorous bombs and incendiaries. Before she left, the American lady laid out in the little air-raid shelter in the garden all the essentials for this act of mercy: a large glass jar of chloroform, the muslin nets with which to catch the birds, and about a hundred masks, each with a small pad in the bottom to be soaked in the anaesthetic.

The first two or three years of war passed off quite well for Capri. The sky above was constantly filled with squadrons, formations, clouds of American bombers, but the island was never touched. Rumour had it that the American lad was very influential at Washington, and had drawn the President's attention to the existence of the birds in her Villa on Capri, and that Roosevelt had promised... What is certain is that, though the Americans showered all the rest of Italy with bombs, they never dropped one on Capri.

Unfortunately, we had also to reckon with Britain. From 10 June 1940, when Mussolini, suddenly breaking the traditional, age-old friendship between the two countries, declared war on Britain, and the Fascists began to shout at the tops of their voices: "Down with England!" we all felt the British were no longer to be relied upon. After the bitter naval engagements in the Mediterranean, the sinking of the fleet at Taranto, and the terrifying bombardment of Genoa, there came in 1943, the landings in Sicily, and there was a great stirring of fleets in the Mediterranean. The possibility of naval attacks began to be envisaged; and these would present a particular danger, as the villa of the birds was on the south side of the island, facing the open sea.

During the three years of war which had passed, the birds had already been decimated by death from natural causes; many had died through the bad quality and the scarcity of bird-food. But there were still about fifty left, and, whatever happened, I had to spare them the horrors of the big naval guns. By the end of the summer the situation was serious; at the beginning of September we began to hear the sound of gunfire, drawing ever nearer. A little after midday on 8 September came a series of piercing blasts on the air-raid siren: one, two, three... five an air-raid? No such luck! six, seven, eight...

There was no doubt what this meant: naval bombardment. On the Anacapri side we felt reasonably safe, for apart from Torre Materita, with Munthe's art-treasures, which the Allies would surely spare, there was a gun-emplacement with a long-range ten-inch gun, the glorious remains of a warship dismantled to provide naval artillery for coastal defence. But at Capri we were in a bad way: only one nest of machine-guns below Punta Tragara, a few shallow trenches on the shore, and some barbed-wire entanglements; and a lot of use they would have been against the fire of the big naval guns.

I felt that the hour had come to fulfil my promise. With the custodian of the villa and an old gardener who looked after the aviary, I began my preparations for the lethal task. Towards two o'clock in the afternoon, as the first light cruisers were sighted, we began to chloroform the South African doves. When we moved on to the Japanese nightingales, the first flotilla of destroyers was already streaking in from the west. Then the outline of the battle-cruisers, fore-runners of the main battle-fleet behind, appeared on the horizon; and hurriedly catching in our nets the few remaining tropical songbirds, we finished our task.

By four o'clock the British and American fleets were lined up opposite Capri from the Gulf of Salerno right up to the island of Ischia, the greatest display of naval strength the world has ever seen. Nobody could understand why the bombardment didn't start straight away.

The last birds to be sacrificed were "Guaio" and "Sventura", a pair of blue and yellow macaws from

Brazil. For years, these two magnificent parrots had been expected to mate, as they do sometimes in captivity, if properly looked after. And in fact at the beginning of September, they had built a nest, and Sventura, separated from Guaio for safety's sake, had already laid an egg. Too late! My promise to the American lady was total, unconditional: at the first signs of an attack, chloroform.

Sventura went to sleep as soon as she was put in the mask, and died peacefully. Guaio must have smelt the anaesthetic, for he struggled a bit, before curling up and dying on the operating table. While he was dying the sirens sounded the all-clear. Shortly afterwards the wireless announced that an Armistice had been signed.

On the night of 8-9 September 1943, the entire German air strength, the most formidable force of bombers she ever put together for a single operation, attacked the Anglo-American naval forces, and Capri, calm, impassive, *au delà de la melée*, witnessed a pyrotechnic display of appalling magnificence.

In its three thousand years of history, the island had been invaded and conquered by Laestrigonians and Teleboans, Greeks and Romans; for a thousand years it had been threatened by the Saracens, who on more than one occasion had devastated and terrorised it. After A.D. 1000 the descent of the Northerners began, and Capri had passed from one foreign rule to another, from the Normans to the Hohenstaufens, from the Hohenstaufens to the Angevins, from the Angevins to the Aragonese, from the Aragonese to the Austrians, from the Austrians to the Spaniards, from the Spaniards to the Bourbons. Finally, with the unity of Italy, Capri had become international. And thus the Americans found it, when they disembarked there, in the middle of September 1943. The island, now became one large Rest Camp, and seethed with a certain frantic madness—drinks, chewing gum, shoeshine, jazz, señorinas, jitterbug, yankee-doodle. And such were the high spirits of the newcomers that from time to time, in the general hilarity, even the tyres of the jeeps burst.

Fifty years ago, when the ferryboat was due, Booth Tarkington used to have himself locked up in the little cell at the foot of the campanile, then the island's prison (and now the guard-room of the local constabulary) and pretend that he had been sent to gaol for his bad conduct.

People used to find these innocent diversions funny, foreigners, that is, not the islanders, for they do not bother about the peculiar behaviour of strangers, nor are they impressed by celebrities of foreign manufacture. After the First World War, a wave of revolutionary artists and *avant-garde* writers came to Capri to form their coteries and schools. It was from Capri that Marinetti declared war on moonlight, and preached the gospel of Futurism, his faith renewed after the enthusiasm, and the derision, encountered in Milan, Paris and Rome. At Capri no-one derided him, nobody became enthusiastic; when he spoke of abolishing the Faraglioni, nobody was alarmed. Instead, everyone said: "*Com'è simpatico, che pazzaglione!*". (*Pazzaglione*, madman, is the honorary title conferred by the Capresi on those who succeed in amusing them).

Then there was the Marchesa Casati, who after stunning Venice with her gilded Moor, and shocking Paris by taking a panther down the Champs Elysées on a lead, came to live in the Villa San Michele—the only person ever to do so—driving Axel Munthe to despair by threatening to replace all the old rubbish in the villa with works by Cubist and Dadaist painters. At Capri she tried to surpass herself. But when she appeared in the Piazza leading a lion-cub on a chain, wearing a tigerskin and preceded by a Chinese servant carrying on his head a glass bowl containing a sacred fish of Siam, the Capresi did not even stop to look at her; at most

199

one or two people, moved to compassion, said: "*Puverella, è furastera!* Poor woman, she's a foreigner!".

This is the spirit which animates the islanders. Perhaps they resent the fact that their old village hall is now taken over by visitors, and their fine Campanile is all festooned with hideous electric lights, that in place of the old shops, so picturesque and colourful, there are now cafés and bars, and stores selling the rubbish which passes as the produce of Capri. But then they remember that the diverting Babel into which the foreigners have turned the island is the very source of Capri's prosperity, and they resign themselves to the inevitable.

And so, even though the characters change, the scene of Capri is still the same. The cafés which once welcomed Gerhart Hauptmann, Gorky, Compton Mackenzie, Hugh Walpole, Francis Brett Young, Louis Golding, now entertain Jean Paul Sartre, Graham Greene, Thornton Wilder, Curzio Malaparte and others.

Up to the First World War, Capri possessed, in Old Spadaro, who taught Lenin to fish, a picturesque example of the local fisherman, sailor and astrologer. He must have been the most photographed man in the world, for his picture can still be seen on old postcards. But today we have gone one better: we have Julius Hans Spiegel. Thirty years ago, after graduating from the School of the Berlin Deaf and Dumb Institute, he toured the principal capitals of Europe as a dancer from Java, or Bali, or Ceylon (it varied from place to place), arousing great enthusiasm. At Rome, his dances (never before seen in Java, or Bali, or Ceylon) sent Marinetti and the futurists into raptures. But his fame waned rapidly, and when he came to Capri, he was already a forgotten man. He took advantage of the complete obscurity into which he had sunk to obtain a livelihood. He began by fitting himself out in a suitable costume, a costume, how can I describe it?—but surely it is known throughout the whole world by now, Spiegel's costume? Large Mexican sombrero, earrings, pipe (unlit), necklace with mysterious amulets, Andalusian bolero, pirate's sash, American jeans, embroidered pockets, innumerable strings of jade, flints, pieces of Oriental pottery, bracelets, rings. Thus attired, and ready for the cameras, he launched the industry of his own autographs, which were sought after avidly by foreigners, sent through the post, sold in the shops. Within two or three years his ever-growing sales made him famous, so that now he does not part so easily with his autographs, but collects those of others—of celebrities he has outstripped.

Spiegel is also one of our better-known painters. When it is time for him to paint, he sets up his easel, rests on it a newly begun picture, and begins to paint—but not like a normal sort of artist. Spiegel paints only unfinished works.

Here one should perhaps commemorate the life and works of the prince of modern visitors to Capri, Norman Douglas. But the task was performed by Douglas himself during his lifetime, in a copious literary production which is almost all autobiographical, and which runs from *Siren Land*, one of his earliest works, to *Looking Back*.

Douglas died in 1952, and now reposes in the little non-Catholic cemetery of Capri, in the diverting company of some of the characters he immortalised in his books.

Much life goes on behind the Piazza, far from the hotels and the centre of the village, in areas of which the curious foreigner does not even suspect the existence. Behind the mask which the island itself wears, there lies its genuine countenance, age-old and noble—the Capri of the Capresi. There are still people who live by the sweat of their brow in the fields and on the sea. But the race of peasants which inspired the idyll of

Gregorovius, tenaciously creating out of the rock-strewn land the terraced fields of Anacapri, Monte Tiberio and Matermania, they, perhaps, have vanished. So, too, have the fishermen of Von Platen's famous eclogue, who in winter passed their storm-tossed existence in the Bocca Grande, on the "Sea of the Garfish", or with their drag-nets swept the bottom of the Secca delle Vedove. At the beginning of the summer they would make their votive offering at the sanctuary of Cetrella, bring their boats to the Grande Marina to be blessed, and leave for the coast of Africa to fish for coral. A large number of fishermen still follow their trade, especially in the squid-fishing season, and during the shoaling season of certain other fish, such as small tunny, bonito, mackerel, gar-fish, sardines and anchovies. From the farms of Anacapri and those of the region of Tiberio come vegetables, especially early ones, for the local market. The days of the Capri shepherd are over; and so are those of the free pasturing of goats. The raising of livestock is now carried on entirely under cover.

The tourist trade, which absorbs so much labour in hotels, cafés and bars, has encouraged or created small local crafts, skilful and flourishing, which produce shoes, sandals, ready-made clothes, and in particular women's garments, which aspire to create a Capri style. Among the most sought-after local products we must also include hand-woven cloth.

In the second half of the nineteenth century, in addition to the artists, and to the writers and historians who made their contribution to the island's literature, Capri was visited by many eminent naturalists. To Italian scientists, and to a large number of foreign zoologists, botanists, geologists and other scholars, among whom were many amateurs, are due many interesting researches and a vast collection of studies concerning the island. These activities, however, came to an end at the beginning of this century.

For some years a small private museum had existed on Capri, containing a collection of minerals, fossils and marine and extramarine molluscs, and also Palaeolithic and Neolithic remains from the various prehistoric stations discovered on the island. To this was attached the Biblioteca Caprense, with its bibliographical material, its archives and its collection of iconography, and the tiny institute, completed by further natural-history collections, obtained official recognition in 1949, and by a decree of the President of the Republic became the *Centro Caprese di Vita e di Studi*. The institute is housed in a group of buildings in Capri, and comprises rooms for art exhibitions, a small theatre, a concert hall, permanent homes for the various collections, and the library. In addition the Centro Caprese owns the Casa Orlandi in Anacapri and the Casa Cetrella, on Monte Solaro. This body numbers among its members many scholars and specialists, who have worked on the geology of the island, who have undertaken excavations of its archaeological remains, and in whose care is the preservation of these and other ancient monuments.

In recent years the Institute, taking advantage of the peculiarly favourable conditions which Capri offers for astronomical observations, has contributed to the establishment of observatories for the study astrophysics, and in particular of solar physics. The Casa Orlandi in Anacapri and the Casa Cetrella on Mont Solaro have been placed at the disposal of the Royal Swedish Academy of Sciences, who have created two important stations for the observation of solar activity. The originator and founder of the Swedish solar station on Capri is Professor Yngve Öhman, who is famous for his researches and discoveries in the fields of stellar astronomy and solar physics. Another "sun-tower" or small observatory has been built at Damecuta, by Professor K.O. Kiepenheuer, the director of the famous Fraunhofer Institute of Freiburg.

Because of its geographical position and climate, Capri possesses conditions particularly favourable for stellar observation. The presence of water on all sides ensures that the atmosphere is clear, free from dust, and calm, except in rare periods of unusually bad weather. The absence of up-currents, even on the hottest days, gives a stable solar image, without vibrations or scintillations, and enables the scientists to record the prominences of the corona, follow the genesis of the sun-spots, or watch the terrifying spectacle of solar eruptions, without disturbances or interruptions.

Before the foreigners came to Capri the Piazza was called Largo di Santo Stefano. In the middle grew an enormous mulberry tree, under which the "public parliaments" were held, and the Commissioners of Provisions, the *Signori della Grascia*, met to provide for the island's food supply. But the Largo was also the parlour of the islanders, and the Piazza has preserved the old trappings of this provincial habit, which comes back into fashion from time to time, and always finds new friends. On two sides, in feigned protection of the population, stretch the arms of the Town Hall— formerly the Bishop's palace, on to which, with the collapse of the Church's temporal power, the State, in triumph, affixed a façade in "King Humbert" style, a manner at once banal and patriotic, which has gone out of fashion, now that the Monarchy has fallen. The arch which connected the Bishopric to the Church now unites Church and Commune—but the Church dominates, looking down on the Town Hall from above, from the top of its magnificent flight of steps, which serves as auditorium for the spectators, when they are not on stage. Facing the Church are the Case Grandi, which have grown up round the little palace where

Joanna of Anjou used to stay. The Queen often came to Capri to distribute alms to the poor and grant privileges to the Carthusians, in expiation of the sins she committed at Naples. In the distance can be glimpsed the magnificent rock curtain of Monte Solaro, which hides Capri from the outside world. Beyond there glitters a little strip of watered silk, just a touch of blue from the Bay. Then finally we come to the *pièce de résistance* of the theatrical decorations: the Clock Tower. Admittedly it is not the Campanile of Venice, nor the Leaning Tower of Pisa, nor Big Ben, nor the Empire State Building. It is simply the Campanile of Capri, not stumpy, like certain belfries with big ideas, nor too tall, like belltowers aping the Campanile of Siena; just a sensible, normal tower of proper height, with a little spherical dome on top, flattened just in time to prevent one thinking of the Arabs. It gives the impression of being moulded by hand—with that final touch which the masons of long ago, throwing aside their trowels, used to give to the junctions of the vaults, to round them off and soften their appearance—in a word, to make them "eye-sweet".

But today it is no longer as it was—a little shabby in appearance, its complexion bronzed by the sun, its plaster bearing that patina which only time can give, the handsome round face of the clock devoid of hands—so friendly, so characteristic of Capri, that the sight of it used to bring tears to our eyes. Today it has been restored, with reinforced concrete, and for many years now the clock, once more working and provided with hands, can tell the time, like any other tower clock. About a century ago, when the hands fell off through old age, it was decided not to replace them, and for a long time the Campanile clock showed all the hours, without pointing to any one in particular; an eternal hour, the time of Capri, which never passes.

Once upon a time the Campanile was joined to a

little church of modest pretensions situated at the entrance to the village, but this was demolished in the seventeenth century. Now, left on its own, it gazes on the nearby pro-Cathedral, showy and enticing, and is not, as it seems, indifferent. Something of the newer building's charm has entered into its old stones, stirring its sentimental old heart. And indeed there is something very enchanting about the handsome façade of the pro-Cathedral, no longer young, it is true, but nevertheless pleasing in its maturity, with its healthy, substantial frame, its well-preserved dome, without a wrinkle of asphalt; and still so ingenuous, that if surprised by the dawn in conversation with the Campanile, it is suffused with blushes...

But few disturb its privacy, nobody is present at the awakening of the church, which stretches its limbs amid the twirligigs and scrolls of the façade, and then settles down to watch, amused but dignified, the show which is shortly to begin in the Piazza. A show which never ends, beginning all over again with each succeeding day. So as not to interrupt, the clock on the Campanile, having no other course open to it, stops. It is almost always stopped now, and from the top of the Campanile gazes down in silence on the Piazza, and on the men and women who pass.

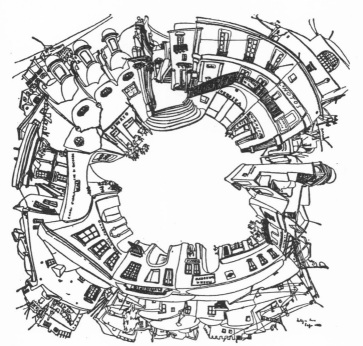

The Piazza

FINITO DI STAMPARE NEL MESE DI MARZO MM
NELLO STABILIMENTO «ARTE TIPOGRAFICA» S.A.S.
S. BIAGIO DEI LIBRAI - NAPOLI